Dictionary of Selected Legal Terms

Third Edition

Revised and Updated by
Margaret C. Jasper

Oceana's Legal Almanac Series:
Law for the Layperson

Oceana®
NEW YORK

OXFORD

UNIVERSITY PRESS

Oxford University Press, Inc., publishes works that further Oxford University's objective of excellence in research, scholarship, and education.

Copyright © 2009 by Oxford University Press, Inc.
Published by Oxford University Press, Inc.
198 Madison Avenue, New York, New York 10016

Library of Congress Cataloging-in-Publication Data

Jasper, Margaret C.
  Dictionary of selected legal terms / by Margaret C. Jasper.—3rd ed., rev. and updated.
       p. cm.—(Oceana's legal almanac series: law for the layperson)
  Includes bibliographical references.
  ISBN 978-0-19-537657-9 ((hardback) : alk. paper)
  1. Law—United States—Dictionaries. I. Title.
  KF156.J37 2009
  340.03—dc22

                                                              2008046771

Note to Readers:
This publication is designed to provide accurate and authoritative information in regard to the subject matter covered. It is based upon sources believed to be accurate and reliable and is intended to be current as of the time it was written. It is sold with the understanding that the publisher is not engaged in rendering legal, accounting, or other professional services. If legal advice or other expert assistance is required, the services of a competent professional person should be sought. Also, to confirm that the information has not been affected or changed by recent developments, traditional legal research techniques should be used, including checking primary sources where appropriate.

(Based on the Declaration of Principles jointly adopted by a Committee of the American Bar Association and a Committee of Publishers and Associations.)

You may order this or any other Oxford University Press publication by visiting the Oxford University Press website at www.oup.com

To My Husband Chris

Your love and support

are my motivation and inspiration

To My Sons, Michael, Nick and Chris

-and-

In memory of my son, Jimmy

ABOUT THE AUTHOR

MARGARET C. JASPER is an attorney engaged in the general practice of law in South Salem, New York, concentrating in the areas of personal injury and entertainment law. Ms. Jasper holds a Juris Doctor degree from Pace University School of Law, White Plains, New York, is a member of the New York and Connecticut bars, and is certified to practice before the United States District Courts for the Southern and Eastern Districts of New York, the United States Court of Appeals for the Second Circuit, and the United States Supreme Court.

Ms. Jasper has been appointed to the law guardian panel for the Family Court of the State of New York, is a member of a number of professional organizations and associations, and is a New York State licensed real estate broker operating as Jasper Real Estate, in South Salem, New York.

Margaret Jasper maintains a website at http://www.JasperLawOffice.com.

In 2004, Ms. Jasper successfully argued a case before the New York Court of Appeals, which gives mothers of babies who are stillborn due to medical negligence the right to bring a legal action and recover emotional distress damages. This successful appeal overturned a 26-year old New York case precedent, which previously prevented mothers of stillborn babies to sue their negligent medical providers.

Ms. Jasper is the author and general editor of the following legal almanacs:

AIDS Law (3d Ed.)

The Americans with Disabilities Act (2d Ed.)

Animal Rights Law (2d Ed.)

Auto Leasing

Bankruptcy Law for the Individual Debtor

Banks and their Customers (3d Ed.)

Becoming a Citizen

Buying and Selling Your Home

Commercial Law

Consumer Rights Law

Co-ops and Condominiums: Your Rights and Obligations As An Owner

Credit Cards and the Law (2d Ed.)

Custodial Rights

Dealing with Debt

Dictionary of Selected Legal Terms (2d Ed.)

Drunk Driving Law

DWI, DUI and the Law

Education Law

Elder Law (2d Ed.)

Employee Rights in the Workplace (2d Ed.)

Employment Discrimination Under Title VII (2d Ed.)

Environmental Law (2d Ed.)

Estate Planning

Everyday Legal Forms

Executors and Personal Representatives: Rights and Responsibilities

Guardianship, Conservatorship and the Law

Harassment in the Workplace

Health Care and Your Rights Under the Law

Health Care Directives

Hiring Household Help and Contractors: Your Obligations Under the Law

Home Mortgage Law Primer (2d Ed.)

Hospital Liability Law (2d Ed.)

How To Change Your Name

How To Form an LLC

How To Protect Your Challenged Child

How To Start Your Own Business

Identity Theft and How To Protect Yourself

Individual Bankruptcy and Restructuring (2d Ed.)

Injured on the Job: Employee Rights, Worker's Compensation and Disability

Insurance Law

International Adoption

Juvenile Justice and Children's Law (2d Ed.)

Labor Law (2d Ed.)

Landlord-Tenant Law

Law for the Small Business Owner (2d Ed.)

The Law of Adoption

The Law of Attachment and Garnishment (2d Ed.)

The Law of Buying and Selling (2d Ed.)

The Law of Capital Punishment (2d Ed.)

The Law of Child Custody

The Law of Contracts

The Law of Copyright (2d Ed.)

The Law of Debt Collection (2d Ed.)

The Law of Alternative Dispute Resolution (2d Ed.)

The Law of Immigration (2d Ed.)

The Law of Libel and Slander

The Law of Medical Malpractice (2d Ed.)

The Law of No-Fault Insurance (2d Ed.)

The Law of Obscenity and Pornography (2d Ed.)

The Law of Patents

The Law of Personal Injury (2d Ed.)

The Law of Premises Liability (2d Ed.)

The Law of Product Liability (2d Ed.)

The Law of Special Education (2d Ed.)

The Law of Speech and the First Amendment

The Law of Trademarks

The Law of Violence Against Women (2d Ed.)

Lemon Laws

Living Together: Practical Legal Issues

Marriage and Divorce (3d Ed.)

Missing and Exploited Children: How to Protect Your Child

More Everyday Legal Forms

Motor Vehicle and Traffic Law

Nursing Home Negligence

Pet Law

Prescription Drugs

Privacy and the Internet: Your Rights and Expectations Under the Law (2d Ed.)

Probate Law

Protecting Your Business: Disaster Preparation and the Law

Real Estate Law for the Homeowner and Broker (2d Ed.)

Religion and the Law

Retirement Planning

The Right to Die (2d Ed.)

Rights of Single Parents

Small Claims Court

Social Security Law (2d Ed.)

Teenagers and Substance Abuse

Transportation Law: Passenger Rights & Responsibilities

Trouble Next Door: What To Do With Your Neighbor

Veterans' Rights and Benefits

Victim's Rights Law

Welfare: Your Rights and the Law

What If It Happened to You: Violent Crimes and Victims' Rights

What if the Product Doesn't Work: Warranties & Guarantees

Workers' Compensation Law (2d Ed.)

Your Child's Legal Rights: An Overview

Your Rights in a Class Action Suit

Your Rights as a Tenant

Your Rights Under the Family and Medical Leave Act

You've Been Fired: Your Rights and Remedies

INTRODUCTION

A common complaint among non-lawyers is understanding the difficult language a lawyer uses in drafting legal documents and explaining the law. This "language" has been referred to as "legalese," and is often frustrating, as well as unnecessary. There have been attempts to transform many legal documents, such as residential leases and mortgage notes, into "plain language" documents to limit confusion; however, for the most part, this complicated legal language remains.

The Legal Almanac Series is designed to provide the non-lawyer with straightforward information on pertinent and timely legal issues and subject matter. The *Dictionary of Selected Legal Terms* is also intended to reduce the complexity of legal definitions by providing clear and simple meanings for commonly used terms covering a wide variety of legal topics. The terms incorporated in the *Dictionary of Selected Legal Terms* were chosen specifically for this purpose, and the definitions have been prepared with the layperson in mind. The goal of the *Dictionary of Selected Legal Terms* is to be a valuable resource for both non-lawyers and lawyers.

DICTIONARY OF SELECTED LEGAL TERMS

A

Abandonment—Knowing relinquishment of one's right or claim to property without any future intent in regaining title or possession.

Abandonment of Child—Refers to a situation where the child's parents have willfully forsaken all parental rights, obligations and claims to the child, as well as all control over and possession of the child, without intending to transfer, or without transferring these rights to any specific person(s).

Abandonment of Spouse—A ground for divorce. Abandonment occurs when the defendant has willfully left the plaintiff continuously, usually for a period of one year or more, without the plaintiff's consent.

Abatement—A lessening, a reduction; also a complete termination of a cause of action.

Abatement of Taxes—A rebate or diminution of taxes previously assessed and/or paid.

Abduction—The criminal or tortious act of taking and carrying away by force.

Abeyance—An undetermined or incomplete state of affairs.

Abolish—To repeal or revoke, such as a law or custom.

Abortion—The premature termination of a pregnancy.

Abrogate—To annul, destroy, revoke, or cancel; the legislative repeal of a law.

Abscond—To secrete oneself from the jurisdiction of the courts.

Abstention—A policy adopted by the federal courts whereby the district court may decline to exercise its jurisdiction and defer to a state court the resolution of a federal constitutional question, pending the outcome in a state court proceeding.

Abstract of Record—An abbreviated form of the case as found in the record.

Abstract of Title—A short history of title to land that contains a record of all conveyances, transfers or other facts relied on as evidence of ownership.

Abuse and Neglect—Physical, sexual and/or emotional maltreatment.

Abuse of Discretion—A standard of review.

Abuse of Process—The improper and malicious use of the criminal or civil process.

Acceleration Clause—A common provision of a mortgage or note providing the holder with the right to demand that the entire outstanding balance is immediately due and usually payable in the event of default.

Acceptance—Acceptance refers to one's consent to the terms of an offer, which consent creates a contract.

Acceptance of Deed—The physical taking of the deed by the grantee.

Acceptance of Offer—The seller's agreement to the terms of the agreement of sale.

Accommodation—A term used in the context of public accommodations and facilities that an individual with a disability may not be excluded, denied services, segregated or otherwise treated differently than other individuals by a public accommodation or commercial facility.

Accord and Satisfaction—Accord and satisfaction refers to the payment of money, or other thing of value, which is usually less than the amount owed or demanded, in exchange for extinguishment of the debt.

Accreditation—A facility gains accreditation when it meets certain quality standards.

Accrue—To occur or come into existence.

Accrued Interest—Interest earned but not yet paid.

Accusation—An indictment, presentment, information or any other form in which a charge of a crime or offense can be made against an individual.

Accusatory Instrument—The initial pleading that forms the procedural basis for a criminal charge, such as an indictment.

Accuse—To directly and formally institute legal proceedings against a person, charging that he or she has committed an offense.

Acknowledgement—A formal declaration of one's signature before a notary public.

Acquiescence—Conduct that may imply consent.

Acquired Citizenship—Citizenship conferred at birth on children born abroad to a U.S. citizen parent.

Acquit—A verdict of "not guilty" which determines that the person is absolved of the charge and prevents a retrial pursuant to the doctrine of double jeopardy.

Acquittal—One who is acquitted receives an acquittal, which is a release without further prosecution.

Act—Legislation passed by Congress.

Act of God—Manifestation of the forces of nature that are unpredictable and difficult to anticipate, such as lightening and earthquakes.

Action at Law—A judicial proceeding whereby one party prosecutes another for a wrongdoing.

Actionable—Giving rise to a legal cause of action.

Actionable Negligence—The breach or nonperformance of a legal duty through neglect or carelessness, resulting in damage or injury to another.

Active Euthanasia—The inducement of gentle death solely by means without which life would continue naturally.

Activities of Daily Living—Impairments are generally defined as conditions which interfere with a person's "activities of daily living," including: (1) self-care and personal hygiene; (2) communication; (3) physical activity; (4) sensory function; (5) hand functions; (6) travel; (7) sexual function; (8) sleep; and (9) social and recreational activities.

Actual Damages—Actual damages are those damages directly referable to the breach or tortious act, and which can be readily proven to have been sustained, and for which the injured party should be compensated as a matter of right.

Actuary—One who computes various insurance and property costs, and calculates the cost of life insurance risks and insurance premiums.

Ad Damnum Clause—The clause in a complaint that sets forth the amount of damages demanded.

Ad Valorem Tax—A tax assessed according to the value of the property.

ADA—The Americans With Disabilities Act (42 USC 12101 et seq.).

Additur—An increase by the court in the amount of damages awarded by the jury.

Adhesion Contract—A standardized contract form offered to consumers of goods and services on a "take it or leave it" basis without affording the consumer a realistic opportunity to bargain, and under such conditions that infer coercion.

Adjourn—To briefly postpone or delay a court proceeding.

Adjudication—The determination of a controversy and pronouncement of judgment.

Adjudicatory Hearing in Juvenile Justice Law—The process by which it is determined whether the allegations in a petition can be proven and, if so, whether they fall within the jurisdictional categories of the juvenile court.

Adjustable Rate Mortgage Loan (ARM)—A loan with an interest rate that is adjusted periodically based on changes in a pre-selected index.

Adjustment Interval—Refers to the time between changes in the interest rate or monthly payment on an adjustable rate mortgage loan.

Adjustment of Status—Refers to the procedure for changing an alien's status from nonimmigrant to immigrant.

Administrative Claim—A claim which takes priority in payment over any pre-petition claims in a pending bankruptcy case.

Administrative Law—Law created by administrative agencies by way of rules, regulations, orders, and decisions.

Administrative Law Judge—The presiding officer at an administrative hearing.

Administrator—The person appointed by the court to settle the estate of a deceased person if he or she dies intestate.

Admiralty Courts—Tribunals exercising jurisdiction over maritime matters.

Admissible Evidence—Evidence that may be received by a trial court to assist the trier of fact, either the judge or jury, in deciding a dispute.

Admission—In criminal law, the voluntary acknowledgment that certain facts are true. In immigration law, refers to a person's entry into the United States, authorized by a Department of Homeland Security, Customs and Border Protection (CBP) officer.

Adopted Child—An unmarried child under age 21, who was adopted while under the age of sixteen, and who has been in the legal custody and lived with the adopting parent(s) for at least two years.

Adoptee—An adopted person.

Adoption—Legal process pursuant to state statute in which a child's legal rights and duties toward his natural parent(s) are terminated, and similar rights and duties toward his adoptive parents are substituted.

Adoption Agency—An organization, usually licensed by the State, that provides services to birth parents, adoptive parents, and children who need families. Agencies may be public or private, secular or religious, for profit or nonprofit.

Adoption Attorney—A legal professional who has experience with filing, processing, and finalizing adoptions in a court having jurisdiction.

Adoption Petition—The legal document through which prospective parents request the court's permission to adopt a specific child.

Adult—An individual who has attained the age of majority.

Adult Adoption—The adoption of a person over the age of majority.

Adult Protective Services—Agency that investigates and resolves reports of alleged psychological and physical abuse, neglect, self-neglect, or financial exploitation of vulnerable adults.

Adultery—A ground for divorce. Adultery is any sexual act or deviate sexual act with a partner other than the spouse.

Advance Directive—A written document that expresses an individual's preferences and instructions regarding health care in the event the individual becomes incompetent or unable to communicate or loses decision-making abilities.

Advance on the Docket—A change in the order in which an appeal is reviewed and decided from the date when it would normally occur to an earlier date.

Advance Parole—Permission to return to the United States after travel abroad granted by the Department of Homeland Security prior to leaving the United States.

Adversary—Opponent or litigant in a legal controversy or litigation.

Adversary Proceeding—A proceeding involving a real controversy contested by two opposing parties.

Adversary System—The system of trial practice in the United States and some other countries in which each of the opposing or adversary parties has full opportunity to present and establish its opposing contentions before the court.

Adverse Possession—The method of acquiring title to property by occupying it openly, notoriously, exclusively and continuously for the statutorily required period of time.

Adverse Witness—A person called to testify for the other side.

Affiant—One who swears to an affidavit, also known as a deponent.

Affidavit—A sworn or affirmed statement made in writing and signed; if sworn, it is notarized.

Affidavit of Service—An affidavit intended to certify the service of a writ, notice, or other document.

Affiliated—Associated or controlled by the same owner or authority.

Affinity—Related by marriage; family relation from one's spouse's family.

Affirm—An act of declaring something to be true under the penalty of perjury by a person who conscientiously declines to take an oath for religious or other pertinent reasons.

Affirmation—A solemn and formal declaration under penalties of perjury that a statement is true, without an oath.

Affirmative Defense—In a pleading, a matter constituting a defense.

Affirmed—Upheld; agreed with (e.g., the Appellate Court affirmed the judgment of the City Court).

Age Discrimination in Employment Act (ADEA)—A federal law that provides that workers over the age of 40 cannot be arbitrarily discriminated against because of age in connection with any employment decision.

Agency—The relationship between a principal and an agent who is employed by the principal, to perform certain acts dealing with third parties.

Agent—One who represents another, known as the principal.

Agreement of Sale—Contract signed by buyer and seller stating the terms and conditions under which a property will be sold.

Agricultural Worker—As a nonimmigrant class of admission, an alien coming temporarily to the United States to perform agricultural labor or services, as defined by the Secretary of Labor.

Air Carrier Access Act—Statute prohibiting discrimination by air carriers against qualified individuals with physical or mental impairments.

Alien—A foreign national who is not a citizen of the United States.

Allegation—The assertion, declaration, or statement of a party to an action, made in a pleading, setting out what the party expects to prove.

Allege—To assert a fact in a pleading.

Alternate Juror—A juror selected as substitute in case another juror must leave the jury panel.

Alternative Dispute Resolution (ADR)—Methods of resolving disputes without official court proceedings, including mediation and arbitration.

Alternative Documentation—A method of documenting a loan file that relies on information the borrower is likely to be able to provide instead of waiting on verification sent to third parties for confirmation of statements made in the application.

Amend—As in a pleading, to make an addition to, or a subtraction from, an already existing pleading.

American Arbitration Association (AAA)—National organization of arbitrators from whose panel arbitrators are selected for labor and civil disputes.

American Bar Association (ABA)—A national organization of lawyers and law students.

American Civil Liberties Union (ACLU)—A nationwide organization dedicated to the enforcement and preservation of rights and civil liberties guaranteed by the federal and state constitutions.

Americans with Disabilities Act (ADA)—A federal law that prohibits employers from discriminating on the basis of a "qualified" disability, as set forth in the statute.

Americans with Disabilities Act Accessibility Guidelines (ADAAG)— Technical standard for accessible design of new construction or alterations adopted by the Department of Justice for places of public accommodation pursuant to Title III of the ADA.

Amicus Curiae—Latin for "friend of the court," refers to one who gives information to the court on some matter of law that is in doubt.

Amicus Curiae Brief—Brief submitted by one who is not a party to the lawsuit to aid the court in gaining the information it needs to make a proper decision.

Amnesty—A pardon that excuses one of a criminal offense.

Amortization—Repayment of a loan with periodic payments of both principal and interest calculated to payoff the loan at the end of a fixed period of time.

Amortization Schedule—A plan for the payment of an indebtedness where there are partial payments of the principal and accrued interest, at stated periods for a definite time, upon the expiration of which the entire amount is satisfied.

Amortized Mortgage—A mortgage in which repayment is made according to a plan requiring the payment of certain amounts at specified times so that all the debt is repaid at the end of the term.

Anatomical Donation—The act of giving one's organs or tissue to someone else.

Ancillary Relief—Additional or supplemental relief sought in a divorce action, such as custody, child support, etc.

Animal Cruelty—Acts of violence or neglect perpetrated against animals, including overt abuse, dog fighting and cockfighting, and denying companion animals the basic necessities of care, such as food, water or shelter.

Animal Welfare Act—Act passed into law in 1966 that ensures that pets and animals used in research and for exhibition purposes are provided humane care and treatment.

Annual Percentage Rate (APR)—The cost of credit expressed at a yearly rate. The annual percentage rate is often not the same as the interest rate. It is a percentage that results from an equation considering the amount financed, the finance charges, and the term of the loan.

Annualization—Twelve-month projection of income from the date of entitlement to pension, or from the effective date of change in income.

Annuity—An amount paid yearly or at other regular intervals, often at a guaranteed minimum amount. Also, a type of insurance policy in which the policy holder makes payments for a fixed period or until a stated age, and then receives annuity payments from the insurance company.

Annulment—To make void by competent authority.

Answer—In a civil proceeding, the principal pleading on the part of the defendant in response to the plaintiff's complaint.

Anticipatory Breach of Contract—A breach committed before the arrival of the actual time of required performance.

Antitrust Laws—Statutes designed to promote free competition in the market place.

Apparent Agency—Apparent agency exists when one person, whether or not authorized, reasonably appears to a third person to be authorized to act as agent for such other.

Appeal—Resort to a higher court for the purpose of obtaining a review of a lower court decision.

Appeal Rights—The right of the parties to a decision to seek review at a higher level.

Appearance—To come into court, personally or through an attorney, after being summoned.

Appellant—The party who takes an appeal to a higher court.

Appellate Court—A court having jurisdiction to review the law as applied to a prior determination of the same case.

Appellee—The party against whom an appeal is taken.

Apportion—To divide according to the parties' respective interests.

Appraisal—A written estimate of a property's current market value completed by an impartial party with knowledge of the real estate market.

Appraisal Fee—A fee charged by a licensed, certified appraiser to render an opinion of market value as of a specific date.

Appraiser—A professional who conducts an analysis of the property, including sales of similar properties, in order to develop an estimate of the value of the property, known as an appraisal.

Appreciation—An increase in the market value of a home due to changing market conditions and/or home improvements.

Appropriations—Budget authority provided through the congressional appropriation process that permits federal agencies to incur obligations and to make payments.

Arbitration—A process whereby disputes are settled by referring them to a fair and neutral third party, known as an arbitrator.

Arbitration Acts—Federal and state laws that provide for submission of disputes to the process of arbitration.

Arbitration Board—A panel of arbitrators appointed to hear and decide a dispute according to the rules of arbitration.

Arbitration Clause—A clause inserted in a contract providing for compulsory arbitration in case of a dispute as to the rights or liabilities under such contract.

Arbitrator—A private, disinterested person, chosen by the parties to a disputed question for the purpose of hearing their contentions, and awarding judgment to the prevailing party.

Architectural Barriers Act (ABA)—A federal law requiring that buildings and facilities that are designed, constructed or altered with federal funds, or leased by a federal agency, must comply with federal standards for physical accessibility by the disabled.

Arguendo—A position taken for the sake of argument even if that position is later contradicted.

Argument—A discourse set forth for the purpose of establishing one's position in a controversy.

Arm's Length—Refers to the bargaining position of two parties that are unrelated to one another and have no other motivation for dealing other than to transact business in good faith.

Arraign—In a criminal proceeding, to accuse one of committing a wrong.

Arraignment—The initial step in the criminal process when the defendant is formally charged with the wrongful conduct.

Arrears—Payments that are due but not yet paid.

Arrest—To deprive a person of his liberty by legal authority.

Arrival-Departure Card—Also known as Form I-94, Arrival-Departure Record. Form I-94 is a small white card given to all foreign visitors at the port of entry by the Department of Homeland Security, Customs and Border Protection official when they enter the United States. Recorded on this card is the visitor's immigrant classification and the authorized period of stay in the United States.

Asbestos—A toxic material that was once used in housing insulation and fireproofing.

Assault—A willful attempt or threat to harm another person, which causes apprehension in that person.

Assessed Value—The value placed on property for the purpose of taxation.

Assessor—A public official who establishes the value of a property for taxation purposes.

Assets—The entirety of a person's property, either real or personal.

Assignee—An assignee is a person to whom an assignment is made, also known as a grantee.

Assignment—The transfer of ownership, rights, or interests in property by one person, the assignor, to another, the assignee.

Assignment of Lease—The transfer of the lessee's entire interest in, but not liability under, an existing lease to another.

Assignment of Mortgage—A document evidencing the transfer of ownership of a mortgage from one person to another.

Assumable Mortgage—A mortgage loan that can be taken over by the buyer when a home is sold.

Assumption—A method of selling real estate where the buyer of the property agrees to become responsible for the repayment of an existing loan on the property.

Assumption Fee—A fee a lender charges a buyer who will assume the seller's existing mortgage.

Assumption of Risk—The legal doctrine that a plaintiff may not recover for an injury to which he assents.

Asylee—An alien in the United States or at a port of entry who is found to be unable or unwilling to return to his or her country of nationality, or to seek the protection of that country because of persecution or a well-founded fear of persecution.

Asylum—A form of protection that allows individuals who are in the United States to remain in the United States, provided that they meet the definition of a refugee and are not barred from either applying for or being granted asylum.

At Issue—Whenever the parties to a suit come to a point in the pleadings that is affirmed on one side and denied on the other, they are said to be "at issue."

Attachment—The taking of property into legal custody by an enforcement officer.

Attending Physician—The doctor who is the primary caregiver for a particular patient.

Attestation—The act of witnessing an instrument in writing at the request of the party making the same, and subscribing it as a witness.

Attorney General of the United States—The Attorney General represents the United States in legal matters and gives advice and opinions to the President and to the heads of the executive departments of the Government when requested.

Attorney General (States)—The chief legal advisor and law officer to the state government.

Attorney-in-Fact—An attorney-in-fact is an agent or representative of another, given authority to act in that person's name and place pursuant to a document called a "power of attorney."

Attorney of Record—Attorney whose name appears in the permanent records or files of a case.

Automatic Stay—An injunction that automatically stops lawsuits, foreclosures, garnishments, and all collection activity against the debtor the moment a bankruptcy petition is filed.

Award—The final and binding decision of an arbitrator, made in writing and enforceable in court under state and federal statutes.

B

Back Pay—Wages awarded to an employee who was illegally discharged.

Background Check—Verification of the accuracy of the information a job applicant provides a prospective employer on his or her employment application.

Bad Faith—A willful failure to comply with one's statutory or contractual obligations.

Bad Title—A title that is not legally sufficient to transfer property to the purchaser.

Bail—Security, usually in the form of money, which is given to insure the future attendance of the defendant at all stages of a criminal proceeding.

Bail Bond—A document that secures the release of a person in custody.

Bailee—A party who holds property of another for a particular purpose pursuant to agreement.

Bailiff—An attendant of the court.

Bailment—The delivery of personal property to be held in trust for some special purpose.

Bailor—A person who delivers personal property to another to be held in bailment.

Balance Sheet—A financial statement that shows assets, liabilities and net worth as of a specific date.

Balloon Mortgage—Balloon mortgage loans are short-term fixed-rate loans with fixed monthly payments for a set number of years followed by one large final "balloon" payment for all of the remainder of the principal.

Balloon Payment—A final lump sum payment that is due, often at the maturity date of a balloon mortgage.

Banishment—A punishment inflicted upon criminals, by compelling them to leave a country for a specified period of time, or for life.

Bankrupt—The state or condition of one who is unable to pay his debts as they are, or become, due.

Bankruptcy—A legal procedure for resolving debt problems of individuals and businesses pursuant to Title 11 of the U.S. Code.

Bankruptcy Code—The informal name for Title 11 of the U.S. Code.

Bankruptcy Court—Refers to a division of the Federal District Court and/or the bankruptcy judges in regular active service in each district.

Bankruptcy Discharge—A court order that eliminates certain debts owed by the debtor for which the creditor may no longer seek payment.

Bankruptcy Estate—All of the legal and equitable interests in property held by the debtor at the time he or she files the bankruptcy petition.

Bankruptcy Judge—A judicial officer of the United States district court who is the court official with decision-making power over federal bankruptcy cases.

Bankruptcy Mill—A business not authorized to practice law that provides bankruptcy counseling and prepares bankruptcy petitions.

Bankruptcy Petition—A formal request for the protection of the federal bankruptcy laws.

Bankruptcy Plan—A debtor's detailed description of how the debtor proposes to pay creditors' claims over a fixed period of time.

Bankruptcy Trustee—The person, appointed by the bankruptcy judge or selected by the creditors, who takes legal title to the property of the debtor and holds it "in trust" for equitable distribution among the creditors.

Bar—To prohibit; also refers to the members of the legal profession.

Bargain—A voluntary and mutual agreement between two parties for the exchange or purchase of some specified goods.

Bargain and Sale Deed with Covenant—A deed conveying real property with a covenant that warrants title against the grantor's acts.

Bargain and Sale Deed Without Covenant—A deed conveying real property without any covenants warranting title.

Basis—The taxpayer's cost in acquiring an asset.

Bastard—A child born out of wedlock.

Battery—The unlawful application of force to a person from another.

Bearer Paper—Commercial paper that is negotiable upon delivery by the one in possession of it.

Before-Tax Income—Income before taxes are deducted, also referred to as "gross income."

Bench—The court and the judges composing the court collectively.

Bench Warrant—An order of the court empowering the police or other legal authority to seize a person.

Beneficiary—A person who is designated to receive property upon the death of another, such as the beneficiary of a life insurance policy, who receives the proceeds upon the death of the insured.

Bequest—Refers to a gift of personal property contained in a will.

Best Evidence Rule—The rule of law that requires the original of a writing, recording or photograph to be produced in order to prove its authenticity.

Bestiality—The illegal act of sexual intercourse with an animal.

Bid—An offer to buy goods or services at a stated price.

Bifurcated Trial—A case in which the trial of the liability issue in a personal injury or wrongful death case is heard separate from and prior to trial of the damages in question.

Bigamy—The criminal offense of willfully and knowingly contracting a second marriage while the first marriage is still undissolved.

Bilateral Contract—A contract containing mutual promises between the parties to the contract, each being termed both a promisor and a promisee.

Bill—In commercial law, an account for goods sold, services rendered and work done.

Bill of Costs—A written statement of the itemized taxable costs and disbursements.

Bill of Exceptions—A document submitted to a trial court stating, for the record, objections to rulings made and instructions given by the trial judge.

Bill of Lading—In commercial law, the document given to the shipper by the carrier in connection with goods to be transported by the carrier.

Bill of Particulars—A request by a party for an amplification of the pleading to which it relates.

Bill of Rights—The first eight amendments to the U.S. Constitution.

Bill of Sale—A written agreement by which the exchange of personal property is made.

Biometrics—Biologically unique information used to identify individuals, including fingerprints, facial recognition and iris scans.

Birth Parent—A child's biological parent.

Biweekly Payment Mortgage—A mortgage with payments due every two weeks.

Blanket Mortgage—A mortgage that covers more than one parcel of real estate.

Board of Directors—The governing body of a corporation which is elected by the stockholders.

Board of Immigration Appeals—The administrative agency of the U.S. Justice Department established by the U.S. Attorney General to review, on appeal, decisions rendered by immigration judges and district directors on issues concerning immigration.

Bodily Injury—Generally refers to any act, except one done in self-defense, that results in physical injury or sexual abuse.

Boilerplate—Refers to standard language found almost universally in certain documents.

Bona Fide Purchaser—One who pays valuable consideration for a purchase.

Bond—A certificate issued by a company or governmental body which represents a debt owed to the bondholder, who receives interest while the debt is outstanding at a specified rate.

Border Crosser—An alien resident of the United States reentering the country after an absence of less than six months in Canada or Mexico, or a nonresident alien entering the United States across the Canadian border for stays of no more than six months or across the Mexican border for stays of no more than 72 hours.

Border Patrol Agent—The law enforcement official responsible for patrolling the U.S. borders with Mexico and Canada to prevent illegal entry of aliens.

Borrower—Also known as the mortgagor, refers to the individual who applies for and receives funds in the form of a loan and is obligated to repay the loan in full under the terms of the loan.

Boundary Line—The dividing line between two adjacent properties.

Breach of Contract—The failure, without any legal excuse, to perform any promise that forms the whole or the part of a contract.

Breach of Duty—In a general sense, any violation or omission of a legal or moral duty.

Breach of Warranty—An infraction of an express or implied agreement as to the title, quality, content or condition of a thing that is sold.

Bridge Loan—A short-term loan secured by the borrower's current home, that allows the proceeds to be used for building or closing on a new house before the current home is sold, also referred to as a "swing loan."

Brief—A document prepared by the lawyers on each side of a dispute and submitted to the court in support of their arguments, which includes points of law, arguments and legal authorities in support of the position advanced in the brief.

Broker—An individual who brings buyers and sellers together and assists in negotiating contracts for a client.

Building Code—Local regulations that set forth the standards and requirements for the construction, maintenance and occupancy of buildings.

Bulk Sales Act—Statutes designed to prevent the defrauding of a merchant's creditors by the secret bulk sale of substantially all of the merchant's stock.

Bulk Transfer—A type of commercial fraud wherein a merchant transfers all or most of the business, for consideration, without paying creditors from the proceeds of the sale.

Burden of Proof—The duty of a party to substantiate an allegation or issue to convince the trier of fact as to the truth of their claim.

Bureau of Labor Statistics—A division of the U.S. Department of Labor that compiles statistics related to employment.

Bureau of Security and Consular Affairs—The State Department bureau responsible for establishing regulations and policies concerning the issuance of visas.

Business Nonimmigrant—An alien coming temporarily to the United States to engage in commercial transactions which do not involve gainful employment in the United States.

Buydown—An arrangement whereby the property developer or another third party provides an interest subsidy to reduce the borrower's monthly payments, typically in the early years of the loan.

Buydown Account—An account in which funds are held so that they can be applied as part of the monthly mortgage payment as each payment comes due during the period that an interest rate buydown plan is in effect.

Buyer's Market—Market conditions that favor buyers.

C

Calendar—A schedule of matters to be heard in court.

Calendar Call—The calling of matters requiring parties, or their attorneys, to appear and be heard, usually done at the beginning of each court day.

Calendar Number—This number is assigned by the court to an action upon the filing of the final papers with the court.

Call Option—A provision of a mortgage note that allows the lender to require repayment of the loan in full before the end of the loan term. The option may be exercised due to breach of the terms of the loan or at the discretion of the lender.

Cap—A limitation on the amount the interest rate or mortgage payments may increase or decrease on an adjustable rate mortgage.

Capacity—Capacity is the legal qualification concerning the ability of one to understand the nature and effects of one's acts. In mortgage law, capacity refers to the buyer's ability to make their mortgage payments on time, which depends on certain factors, including income, assets and savings, and net income after deducting debts and other obligations.

Capital—Pertaining to corporations, capital refers to all of its money and property used to transact its business.

Capital Crime—A crime for which the death penalty may, but need not necessarily be imposed.

Capital Offense—A criminal offense punishable by death.

Capital Punishment—The penalty of death.

Caption—The heading of a legal document which contains the name of the court, the index number assigned to the matter, and the names of the parties.

Case Administrator—Employee of the American Arbitration Association who is assigned to administer cases.

Case File—The court file containing papers submitted in a case.

Cash Out—Any cash received when you get a new loan that is larger than the remaining balance of your current mortgage, based upon the equity you have already built up in the house. The cash out amount is calculated by subtracting the sum of the old loan and fees from the new mortgage loan.

Cashier's Check—Also known as a bank check, refers to a check whose payment is guaranteed because it was paid for in advance and is drawn on the bank's account instead of the customer's account.

Caucuses—Meetings in which a mediator talks with the parties individually to discuss the issues.

Causation—A factor that contributed to the occurrence of an injury or illness.

Cause of Action—The grounds on which a legal action may be brought, such as property damage, personal injury, contract matters, etc.

Caveat Emptor—Latin for "let the buyer beware."

Cease and Desist Order—A court order prohibiting an unlawful course of conduct or activity.

Ceiling—The maximum allowable interest rate of an adjustable rate mortgage.

Censure—The official reprimand by a legislative or other formal body of one of its own members.

Certificate of Citizenship—A document issued by the Department of Homeland Security as proof that the person is a U.S. citizen by birth or derivation.

Certificate of Deposit—A document issued by a bank or other financial institution that is evidence of a deposit, with the issuer's promise to return the deposit plus earnings at a specified interest rate within a specified time period.

Certificate of Eligibility—Document issued by the Veterans Administration to qualified veterans that verifies a veteran's eligibility for a VA guaranteed loan.

Certificate of Naturalization—A document issued by the Department of Homeland Security as proof that the person has become a U.S. citizen after immigration to the United States.

Certificate of Occupancy—A document issued by local governmental authorities that certifies that a building conforms to local building code regulations.

Certificate of Readiness—A document attesting that the parties in a lawsuit are ready to go to trial.

Certificate of Title—Written opinion of the status of title to a property, given by an attorney or title company. This certificate does not offer the protection given by title insurance.

Certificate of Veteran Status—Federal Housing Authority (FHA) form filled out by the Veterans Administration to establish a borrower's eligibility for an FHA Veteran loan.

Certified Check—A check containing the bank's certification that the drawer of the check has sufficient funds to cover payment of the check, which amount will be retained by the bank until the check is presented for payment.

Certified Copy—Copy of a document signed and certified as a true copy of an original by the Clerk of the Court or other authorized persons.

Certify—To testify in writing.

Certifying Officer—Employee of the United States Labor Department responsible for issuing labor certificates.

Chapter 12

Certiorari—A common law writ whereby a higher court requests a review of a lower court's records to determine whether any irregularities occurred in a particular proceeding.

Chain of Title—The chronological order of conveyance of a property from the original owner to the present owner.

Change of Venue—The removal of a suit begun in one county or district to another county or district for trial, though the term may also apply to the removal of a suit from one court to another court of the same county or district.

Change Status—Changing from one nonimmigrant visa status to another nonimmigrant visa status while a person is in the United States.

Chapter 11—The chapter of the Bankruptcy Code providing for reorganization whereby the debtor usually proposes a plan of reorganization to keep its business alive and pay creditors over time.

Chapter 15—The chapter of the Bankruptcy Code that incorporates the Model Law on Cross-Border Insolvency drafted by the U.N. Commission on International Trade Law (UNCITRAL).

Chapter 9—The chapter of the Bankruptcy Code providing for reorganization of municipalities, including cities, towns, villages, counties, taxing districts, municipal utilities, and school districts.

Chapter 7—The chapter of the Bankruptcy Code providing for the liquidation—i.e., the sale—of a debtor's nonexempt property and the distribution of the proceeds to creditors.

Chapter 13—The chapter of the Bankruptcy Code providing for adjustment of debts of an individual with regular income.

Chapter 12—The chapter of the Bankruptcy Code providing for adjustment of debts of a "family farmer," or a "family fisherman" as those terms are defined in the Bankruptcy Code.

Charge—Under Title VII, refers to a formal allegation filed with the EEOC by a charging party claiming to have been discriminated against by an employer, labor union or employment agency when applying for a job, or on the job because of race, color, religion, sex, or national origin.

Charge-Off—A debt deemed uncollectible by the creditor and reported as a bad debt to a credit reporting agency.

Charge to Jury—In trial practice, an address delivered by the court to the jury at the close of the case instructing the jury as to what principles of law they are to apply in reaching a decision.

Charity—For income tax purposes, a charity is a nonprofit institution organized and operated exclusively for charitable purposes, whose income is exempt from federal income tax.

Charter—The document issued by the government establishing a corporate entity.

Chattel—Any tangible, movable piece of personal property as opposed to real property, such as land.

Chattel Mortgage—A conveyance of some present legal or equitable right in personal property as security for the performance of some act, e.g., the payment of money.

Chattel Paper—A writing which evidences both a monetary obligation and a security interest in specific goods.

Check—A draft drawn upon a bank and payable on demand, signed by the maker or drawer, and containing an unconditional promise to pay a certain sum of money to the payee.

Chief Justice—The presiding member of certain courts that have more than one judge, e.g., the U.S. Supreme Court.

Child—Used to describe a broad category of individuals who are younger than adult.

Child Abuse—Any form of cruelty to a child's physical, moral, or mental well-being.

Child Custody—The care, control and maintenance of a child that may be awarded by a court to one of the parents of the child.

Child Labor Laws—Network of laws on both federal and state levels, prescribing working conditions for children in terms of hours and nature of work that may be performed, all designed to protect the child.

Child Protective Agency—A state agency responsible for the investigation of child abuse and neglect reports.

Child Support—The legal obligation of parents to contribute to the economic maintenance of their children.

Child Welfare—A generic term that embraces the totality of measures necessary for a child's well being; physical, moral, and mental.

Choate—Completed or perfected.

Circuit—A judicial division of a state or the United States.

Circuit Court—One of several courts in a given jurisdiction.

Circumstantial Evidence—Indirect evidence by which a principal fact may be inferred.

Citation—A summons to appear in court; also refers to legal authorities provided in support of an argument.

Civil Action—An action maintained to protect a private, civil right as opposed to a criminal action.

Civil Court—The court designed to resolve disputes arising under the common law and civil statutes.

Civil Disobedience—The refusal to obey a law for the purpose of demonstrating its unfairness.

Civil Disorder—A violent public disturbance involving a group of three or more persons, which causes immediate danger, damage or injury to the property or person of another.

Civil Law—Law that applies to noncriminal actions.

Civil Penalty—A fine imposed as punishment for a certain activity.

Civil Rights Act of 1964—The federal act passed to provide stronger protection for rights guaranteed by the Constitution, such as voting rights.

Civil Rights of Institutionalized Persons Act (CRIPA)—Statute intended to monitor the health and safety of individuals confined in State and local government correctional facilities, nursing homes and mental institutions.

Claim—In a bankruptcy proceeding, a creditor's assertion of a right to payment from a debtor or the debtor's property.

Claimant—In an arbitration proceeding, refers to the party who brings the petition.

Class Action—A lawsuit brought by a representative member of a large group of persons on behalf of all the members of the group.

Clayton Act—A federal statute amending the Sherman Antitrust Act.

Clean Hands Doctrine—The concept that claimants who seek equitable relief must not have indulged in any impropriety in relation to the transaction upon which relief is sought.

Clear and Convincing Evidence—A high measure or degree of proof that may be required in some civil cases.

Clear Title—Ownership that is free of liens, defects, or other legal encumbrances.

Clerk's Extract—A summary of a trial that is written by a clerk.

Clerk's Minutes—Notes, which are taken by a clerk, of events that occurred in court.

Close Corporation—A corporation whose shares, or at least voting shares, are held by a single shareholder or closely-knit group of shareholders.

Closing—Also known as settlement, refers to the conclusion of a real estate transaction and includes the delivery of the security instrument, signing of legal documents, and the disbursement of the funds necessary to the sale of the home or loan transaction.

Closing Agent—The person or entity that coordinates the various closing activities, including the preparation and recordation of closing documents, and the disbursement of funds.

Closing Costs—Also known as settlement costs, refers to the costs for services that must be performed before the loan can be initiated, such as title fee, recording fee, appraisal fee, credit report fee, the pest inspection, attorney's fee, and surveying fee.

Closing Date—The date on which the sale of a property is to be finalized and a loan transaction completed.

Closing Statement—A final listing of the closing costs of the mortgage transaction, including the sale price, down payment, total settlement costs required form the buyer and seller, also referred to as the HUD-1 Settlement Statement.

Co-Borrower—Any borrower other than the first borrower whose name appears on the application and mortgage note.

Co-Maker—One who signs the note of another, either for value or accommodation, and who is thus liable to the payee.

Co-Obligor—One who is bound together with one or more others in a promise to perform or pay a sum of money under a contract.

Co-Signer—A person who signs a promissory note that is also signed by one or more other parties, and for which both parties are responsible for the underlying debt.

Codicil—A document modifying an existing will which, in order to be valid, must be formally drafted and witnessed according to statutory requirements.

Coerce—To compel by pressure, threat, or force.

Coercion—Refers to (a) threats of serious harm to or physical restraint against any person; (b) any scheme, plan, or pattern intended to cause a person to believe that failure to perform an act would result in serious harm to or physical restraint against any person; or (c) the abuse or threatened abuse of the legal process.

Cohabit—To live together without a legal marriage ceremony.

Cohabitation—The mutual assumption of those marital rights, duties, and obligations that are usually manifested by married people.

Collateral—Property that is pledged as additional security for a debt, such as a loan.

Collateral Attack—A challenge to the validity of a prior ruling which is brought in a special proceeding, separate from that in which the ruling was rendered.

Collateral Document—A legal document covering the item(s) pledged as collateral on a loan, i.e., note, mortgages, assignment, etc.

Collateral Estoppel—The legal doctrine recognizing that the determination of facts litigated between two parties in a proceeding is binding on those parties in all future proceedings against each other.

Collective Bargaining—In labor law, refers to the negotiation between employers and employees conducted by a union representative designated by a majority of the employees.

Collective Bargaining Agreement—An agreement between an employer and a labor union which regulates terms and conditions of employment.

Collusion—An agreement with another for the purpose of engaging in an illegal activity.

Color of Law—Refers to an action that appears to be done under lawful authority but is actually against the law.

Color of Title—An instrument which appears to legally pass title but which fails to do so because of some defect.

Comity—Refers to the situation where one court defers to the ruling of another court, as a matter of courtesy and expediency.

Commercial Paper—A negotiable instrument.

Commingle—To combine funds or property into a common fund.

Commingling of Funds—The act of mixing a client's funds with that of a fiduciary, trustee, or lawyer's own funds.

Commission—Compensation for services performed which is based on a percentage of an agreed amount.

Commissioner of Jurors—Person in charge of summoning citizens for jury duty.

Commitment—An order to commit a person to the custody of a sheriff, commissioner of corrections, or mental health facility.

Commitment Letter—A binding offer from a lender that includes the amount of the mortgage, the interest rate, and repayment terms.

Common Areas—Those portions of a building, land, or improvements and amenities owned by a planned unit development or homeowner's association that are used by all of the unit owners who share in the common expenses of their operation and maintenance.

Common Law—Common law is the system of jurisprudence that originated in England and was later applied in the United States.

Common-Law Marriage—One not solemnized in the ordinary way but created by a present agreement to be deemed married from that moment forward, followed by cohabitation.

Community Development Block Grant Program (CDBGP)—A federal program administered by the U.S. Department of Housing and Urban Development (HUD), which provides funding to public entities for the purpose of taking measures to facilitate access for the disabled population to the entity's services and programs.

Community Property—A form of ownership in a minority of states where a husband and wife are deemed to own property in common, including earnings, each owning an undivided one-half interest in the property.

Comparables—Comparable properties that are used as a comparison in determining the current value of a property that is being appraised.

Compensable Injury—An accidental injury arising out of and in the course of employment that requires medical services or results in disability or death.

Compensation—Refers to the benefits payable to claimants under a workers' compensation claim, such as lost wages, medical expenses, etc.

Compensatory Damages—Compensatory damages are those damages directly referable to a breach or tortious act, and which can be readily proven to have been sustained, and for which the injured party should be compensated as a matter of right.

Competent Adult—An adult who is alert, capable of understanding a lay description of medical procedures, and able to appreciate the consequences of providing, withholding, or withdrawing medical procedures.

Competent Authority—A court or governmental agency of a foreign country having jurisdiction and authority to make decisions in matters of child welfare, including adoption.

Complaint—In a civil proceeding, the first pleading of the plaintiff setting out the facts on which the claim for relief is based.

Compromise and Settlement—An arrangement arrived at, either in court or out of court, for settling a dispute upon what appears to the parties to be equitable terms.

Compulsory Arbitration—Arbitration that occurs when the consent of one of the parties is enforced by statutory provisions.

Compulsory Education—The legal obligation to attend school up to a certain age.

Concerted Action—An act that is planned and carried out between parties who are acting together.

Conciliation—The adjustment and settlement of a dispute in a friendly, cooperative manner.

Conclusion of Fact—A conclusion reached by natural inference and based solely on the facts presented.

Conclusion of Law—A conclusion reached through the application of rules of law.

Conclusive Evidence—Evidence that is incontrovertible.

Concurrent—In criminal law, refers to sentences that are to be served simultaneously.

Condition—A future and uncertain event upon the happening of which some obligation is contingent.

Condition Concurrent—A condition concurrent is a condition precedent that exists only when parties to a contract are found to render performance at the same time.

Condition Precedent—A condition precedent is a condition that must occur before the agreement becomes effective, and which calls for the happening of some event before the contract shall be binding on the parties.

Condition Subsequent—A condition subsequent is a provision giving one party the right to divest himself of liability and obligation to perform further if the other party fails to meet the condition.

Condominium—A form of property ownership in which the homeowner holds title to an individual dwelling unit and a proportionate interest in common areas and facilities of a multi-unit project.

Condonation—Conditional forgiveness by one of the married parties, of a known matrimonial offense committed by the other, that would constitute a cause of divorce, as demonstrated by continuation or resumption of marital cohabitation.

Confession—In criminal law, an admission of guilt or other incriminating statement made by the accused.

Confession of Judgment—An admission of a debt by the debtor that may be entered as a judgment without the necessity of a formal legal proceeding.

Confidence Game—A scheme where the perpetrator wins the confidence of his or her victim in order to cheat the victim out of a sum of money or other valuable.

Confidentiality—The legally required process of keeping identifying or other significant information secret; the principle of ethical practice which requires social workers and other professional not to disclose information about a client without the client's consent.

Confiscate—To take private property without just compensation.

Conflict of Law—The body of law by which the court, in which the action is pending, chooses which law to apply in a controversy, where there exists diversity between the applicable law of two jurisdictions, both of which have an interest.

Conforming Loan—A mortgage loan which meets all requirements to be eligible for purchase by federal agencies such as the Federal National Mortgage Association (FNMA a/k/a "Fannie Mae") and the Federal Home Loan Mortgage Corporation (FHLMC a/k/a "Freddie Mac").

Confrontation Clause—A Sixth Amendment right of the Constitution which permits the accused in a criminal prosecution to confront the witness against him.

Consanguinity—Related by blood.

Conscientious Objector—One who, because of religious belief, is opposed to any form of participation in war.

Consecutive—In criminal law, refers to sentences that are to be served in numerical order.

Consent Judgment—An agreement reached by the parties and entered on the record with judicial approval with the same effect as a judgment.

Consent Search—A search that is carried out with the voluntary authorization of the subject of the search.

Consequential Damages—Damages which are caused by an injury, but which are not a necessary result of the injury, and must be specially pleaded and proven in order to be awarded.

Conservatee—An incompetent or incapacitated person placed under the care of a conservator by the court.

Conservator—A conservator is the court-appointed custodian of property belonging to a person determined to be unable to properly manage his or her property.

Conservatorship—A legal relationship between a conservator and a conservatee.

Consideration—Something of value exchanged between parties to a contract, which is a requirement of a valid contract.

Consolidate—A joining of two or more actions to be tried together.

Consolidated Action—Two or more actions involving a common question of law or fact that are consolidated by the court, become one action with one title, and result in one verdict, and one judgment.

Consortium—The conjugal association of husband and wife, and the right of each to the company and care of the other.

Conspiracy—A scheme by two or more persons to commit a criminal or unlawful act.

Conspirator—One of the parties involved in a conspiracy.

Constitution—The fundamental principles of law that frame a governmental system.

Constitutional Right—Refers to the individual liberties granted by the constitution of a state or the federal government.

Constructive Abandonment—A ground for divorce. Constructive abandonment occurs when the defendant has refused to engage in sexual relations with the plaintiff continuously, usually for a period of one year or more, without the plaintiff's consent.

Constructive Discharge—In general, a constructive discharge occurs when a worker's resignation or retirement is found to be involuntary because the employer has created a hostile or intolerable work environment, or has applied other forms of pressure or coercion that forced the employee to quit or resign.

Consumer Bankruptcy—A bankruptcy case filed to reduce or eliminate debts that are primarily consumer debts.

Consumer Credit—Loans and sale credit extended to individuals to finance the purchases of goods and services arising out of consumer needs and desires.

Consumer Credit Counseling Service—A service that offers counseling to consumers and serves as a intermediary with creditors regarding debt repayment and budget planning.

Consumer Debtor—A debtor whose debts are primarily consumer debts.

Consumer Debts—Debts incurred for personal, as opposed to business, needs.

Contempt of Court—An act or omission tending to obstruct or interfere with the orderly administration of justice, or to impair the dignity of the court or respect for its authority.

Contested Divorce—A divorce action that is defended.

Contested Matter—Matters that are disputed but are not within the definition of an adversary proceeding under the bankruptcy rules.

Contingency—A condition that must be satisfied before a contract is legally binding.

Contingency Fee—The fee charged by an attorney, which is dependent upon a successful outcome in the case, and is often agreed to be a percentage of the party's recovery.

Contingent—Conditioned upon the occurrence of some future event.

Contingent Claim—A claim in bankruptcy that may be owed by the debtor under certain circumstances, such as a co-signer.

Contract—A contract is an agreement between two or more persons that creates an obligation to do or not to do a particular thing.

Contract of Sale—The agreement between the buyer and seller on the purchase price, terms, and conditions of a sale.

Contribution—Sharing of a loss or payment among two or more parties.

Contributory Negligence—The act or omission amounting to want of ordinary care on the part of the complaining party which, concurring with the defendant's negligence, is the proximate cause of his or her injury.

Conventional Mortgage—A mortgage made by a financial institution that is not insured or guaranteed by the government.

Conversion—The process by which the court, the debtor, or a creditor in a bankruptcy case pending under one chapter transfers the case to another chapter.

Conversion Clause—A provision in some adjustable rate mortgages (ARM) that allows you to change the ARM to a fixed-rate loan, usually after the first adjustment period. The new fixed rate will be set at current rates, and there may be a charge for the conversion feature.

Convertible Adjustable Rate Mortgage—A type of adjustable rate mortgage (ARM) loan with the option to convert the ARM to a fixed-rate loan during a given time period.

Conveyance—The transfer of property, or title to property, from one person to another, by means of a written instrument and other formalities.

Cooperative—Ownership of stock in a corporation that owns property that is subdivided into individual units.

Copyright—Refers to the legal protection given to the works of authors and artists, granting them exclusive control over the right to publish their works.

Coroner—The public official whose responsibility it is to investigate the circumstances and causes of deaths that occur within his or her jurisdiction.

Corporal Punishment—Physical punishment as distinguished from pecuniary punishment or a fine; any kind of punishment of, or inflicted on, the body.

Corporation—A group of persons granted a state charter legally recognizing them as a separate entity having its own rights, privileges, and liabilities distinct from those of its members.

Corroborate—To add weight by additional evidence.

Cost of Funds Index (COFI)—An index of the weighted-average interest rate paid by savings institutions for sources of funds, usually by members of the 11th Federal Home Loan Bank District.

Costs—A sum payable by the losing party to the successful party for his or her expenses in prosecuting or defending a case.

Counsel—Lawyer or attorney.

Counterclaims—Counterdemands made by a respondent in his or her favor against a claimant.

Counterfeit—Refers to something that is made in imitation of something else for the purposes of defrauding others by passing the false copy for the genuine.

Counteroffer—A statement by the person receiving the offer, that has the legal effect of rejecting the offer, and of proposing a new offer to the person who made the initial offer.

Countersign—The addition of a signature to an instrument to attest its authenticity.

Country of Birth—The country in which a person is born.

Country of Citizenship—The country in which a person is born or naturalized and to which that person owes an allegiance and by which he or she is entitled to be protected.

Country of Former Allegiance—The previous country of citizenship of a naturalized United States citizen or of a person who derived United States citizenship.

Country of Last Residence—The country in which an alien habitually resided prior to entering the United States.

Country of Nationality—The country of a person's citizenship or country in which the person is deemed to be a national.

Court—The branch of government responsible for the resolution of disputes arising under the laws of the government.

Court-Martial—The trial court of the military court's system that is empowered to impose sentences of confinement and/or discharge upon a member of the military for service-connected crimes.

Court of Claims—The federal court created to resolve claims against the United States.

Court of Conciliation—A court that proposes terms of adjustment of a dispute so as to avoid litigation.

Court of Limited Jurisdiction—A city court, district court or other court that has jurisdiction only over actions authorized by law.

Court Reporter—A person who transcribes by shorthand or stenographically takes down testimony during court proceedings.

Covenant—An agreement or promise to do or not to do a particular thing, as to bind oneself in contract.

Credit—The ability of a person to borrow money or buy goods by paying over time.

Credit Bureau—A company that gathers information on consumers who use credit, and then sell that information to lenders and other businesses in the form of a credit report.

Credit Counseling—Generally refers to two events in individual bankruptcy cases: (1) the "individual or group briefing" from a nonprofit budget and credit counseling agency that individual debtors must attend prior to filing under any chapter of the Bankruptcy Code; and (2) the "instructional course in personal financial management" in chapters 7 and 13 that an individual debtor must complete before a discharge is entered.

Credit Life Insurance—A type of insurance that pays off a specific amount of debt or a specified credit account if the borrower dies while the policy is in force.

Credit Insurance—An insurance policy that pays off credit card debt if the borrower loses his or her job, becomes disabled, or dies.

Credit Rating—A judgment of an individual consumer's ability to repay their debts, based on current and projected income and history of payment of past debts.

Credit Report—Refers to the document from a credit reporting agency setting forth a credit rating and pertinent financial data concerning a person or a company, which is used in evaluating the applicant's financial stability.

Credit-Reporting Agency—A business that keeps records of people's credit histories, and that reports credit history information to prospective creditors, including landlords.

Credit Score—A numerical value that ranks a borrower's credit risk.

Creditor—A person who extends credit to whom a debtor owes money.

Creditors' Meeting—The meeting of creditors required by section 341 of the Bankruptcy Code at which the debtor is questioned under oath by creditors, a trustee, examiner, or the U.S. trustee about the debtor's financial affairs.

Criminal Court—The court designed to hear prosecutions under the criminal laws.

Criminal Impersonation—As it pertains to identity theft, means to knowingly assume a false or fictitious identity or capacity, and in that identity or capacity, doing any act with intent to unlawfully gain a benefit or injure or defraud another.

Cross-Claim—A claim litigated by co-defendants or co-plaintiffs against each other and not against a party on the opposite side of the litigation.

Cross-Examination—The questioning of a witness by someone other than the one who called the witness to the stand concerning matters about which the witness testified during direct examination.

Cruel and Inhuman Treatment—A ground for divorce. Cruel and inhuman treatment consists of cruelty, whether physical, verbal, sexual or emotional, committed by the defendant, against the plaintiff, that endangers the plaintiff's well-being and makes living together either unsafe or improper.

Cruel and Unusual Punishment—Refers to punishment that is shocking to the ordinary person, inherently unfair, or excessive in comparison to the crime committed.

Cruelty—The intentional and malicious infliction of physical or mental suffering on one's spouse.

Culpable—Referring to conduct, it is that which is deserving of moral blame.

Cushion—The excess balance a mortgage lender may require a borrower to maintain in their escrow account to cover unanticipated increases in the following year's real estate tax and insurance bills.

Custodial Care—Nonskilled, personal care, such as assistance with activities of daily living.

Customs and Border Protection (CBP)—Agency under the jurisdiction of the Department of Homeland Security that is responsible for admission of all travelers seeking entry into the United States, and determining the length of authorized stay, if the traveler is admitted.

Customs Officer—The law enforcement official responsible for inspecting the luggage, personal effects, and customs declarations of persons arriving in the United States.

D

Damages—In general, damages refers to monetary compensation which the law awards to one who has been injured by the actions of another, such as in the case of tortious conduct or breach of contractual obligations.

Date-Stamp—The stamping on a document of the date it is received by the court.

De Facto—Past act that must be accepted although illegitimate.

De Novo—From the beginning; refers to a new trial.

Death Benefit—The amount of money paid to the surviving spouse of a deceased Social Security beneficiary under certain circumstances.

Death Claim—A claim brought by a deceased employee's surviving dependents due to a work-related injury or illness resulting in the employee's death.

Debenture—Debt instrument evidencing the holder's right to receive interest and principal installments from the named obligor.

Debt—Money owed from one person or institution to another person or institution.

Debt Bondage—The status or condition of a debtor arising from a pledge by the debtor of his or her personal services or of those of a person under his or her control as a security for debt, if the value of those services as reasonably assessed is not applied toward the liquidation of the debt or the length and nature of those services are not respectively limited and defined.

Debt-to-Income Ratio—The percentage of gross monthly income that goes toward paying for the borrower's monthly expenses.

Debtor—A person who has filed a petition for relief under the bankruptcy laws.

Decedent—A deceased person.

Decision—The determination reached by a court in any judicial proceeding, which is the basis of the judgment.

Declaratory Judgment—A judgment that fixes the rights of the parties without ordering anything to be done.

Decree—A decision or order of the court.

Deductible—An amount an insured person must pay before they are entitled to recover money from the insurer, in connection with a loss or expense covered by an insurance policy.

Deed—Legal document by which title to real property is transferred from one owner to another. The deed contains a description of the property, and is signed, witnessed, and delivered to the buyer at closing.

Deed in Lieu of Foreclosure—The transfer of title from a borrower to the lender to satisfy the mortgage debt and avoid foreclosure, also referred to as a voluntary conveyance.

Deed of Trust—A legal document that conveys title to real property to a third party. The third party holds title until the owner of the property has repaid the debt in full.

Defamation—The publication of an injurious statement about the reputation of another.

Default—Failure to meet legal obligations in a contract, such as failure to make payments on a loan.

Default Judgment—A judgment may be obtained against a defendant when the defendant fails to respond to the summons and/or complaint within the time allowed by law.

Defendant—In a civil proceeding, the party responding to the complaint.

Defense—Opposition to the truth or validity of the plaintiff's claims.

Deliberation—The process by which a panel of jurors comes to a decision on a verdict.

Delinquency—Failure to make payments as agreed in the loan agreement.

Delinquent—An infant of not more than a specified age who has violated criminal laws or has engaged in disobedient, indecent or immoral conduct, and is in need of treatment, rehabilitation, or supervision.

Demand for Arbitration—A unilateral filing of a claim in arbitration based on the filer's contractual or statutory right to do so.

Demurrer—A legal response that a tenant can file in an unlawful detainer lawsuit to test the legal sufficiency of the charges made in the landlord's complaint.

Denomination—A religious group or community.

Department of Homeland Security (DHS)—DHS is comprised of three main organizations responsible for immigration policies, procedures, implementation and enforcement of U.S. laws, including the U.S. Citizenship and Immigration Services (USCIS); Customs and Border Protection (CBP); and Immigration and Customs Enforcement (ICE). Together they provide the basic governmental framework for regulating the flow of visitors, workers and immigrants to the United States.

Department of Labor—A cabinet level unit of the U.S. Government that has responsibility for labor issues, and is responsible for deciding whether certain foreign workers can work in the United States.

Departure Under Safeguards—The departure of an illegal alien from the United States which is physically observed by an Immigration and Naturalization Service official.

Deponent—One who testifies under oath to the truth of facts.

Deportable Alien—An alien in and admitted to the United States, subject to any grounds of removal specified in the Immigration and Nationality Act. This includes any alien illegally in the United States, regardless of whether the alien entered the country by fraud or misrepresentation, or entered legally but subsequently violated the terms of his or her nonimmigrant classification or status.

Deportation—The formal removal of an alien from the United States when the alien has been found removable for violating the immigration laws.

Deposition—A method of pretrial discovery that consists of a statement of a witness under oath, taken in question and answer form, as it would be in court, with opportunity given to the adversary to be present and cross-examine.

Depreciation—A decline in the value of a house due to changing market conditions or lack of upkeep on the home.

Derivative Citizenship—Citizenship conveyed to children through the naturalization of parents or, under certain circumstances, to foreign-born children adopted by U.S. citizen parents, provided certain conditions are met.

Derivative Status—Refers to obtaining a status (visa) through another applicant, as provided under immigration law for certain visa categories.

Digital Signature—A digital signature is a digital certification or stamp that uses encryption technology to authenticate an individual's signature is legitimate.

Direct Examination—The first interrogation of a witness by the party on whose behalf the witness is called.

Directed Verdict—An instruction by the judge to the jury to return a specific verdict.

Disability—Under the Americans with Disabilities Act (ADA), an individual is considered disabled if he or she: (i) is substantially impaired with respect to a major life activity; (ii) has a record of such an impairment; or (iii) is regarded as having an impairment.

Disabled Veteran—A veteran who is entitled to compensation under laws administered by the Veterans Administration; or an individual who was discharged or released from active duty because of service connected disability.

Disabling Compensable Injury—An on-the-job injury that entitles the worker to temporary or permanent, partial or total disability compensation or death benefits.

Discharge—A court order that eliminates certain debts owed by the debtor for which the creditor may no longer seek payment.

Dischargeable Debt—A debt for which the Bankruptcy Code allows the debtor's personal liability to be eliminated.

Disclaimer—Words or conduct which tend to negate or limit warranty in the sale of goods, which in certain instances must be conspicuous and refer to the specific warranty to be excluded.

Disclosure—The act of disclosing or revealing that which is secret or not fully understood.

Discount Point—An up-front fee paid to a mortgage lender at the time that the borrower obtains a mortgage loan. Each point equals one percent of the total loan amount. Points and interest rates are inherently connected: in general, the more points the borrower pays, the lower the interest rate. However, the more points one pays, the more cash they need up front since points are paid in cash at closing.

Discount Rate—The discount rate is the percentage of the face amount of commercial paper that a holder pays when he transfers such paper to a financial institution for cash or credit.

Discovery—Modern pretrial procedure by which one party gains information held by another party.

Dismissal—Termination of a proceeding for a procedurally prescribed reason.

Dismissal with Prejudice—Action dismissed on the merits that prevents renewal of the same claim or cause of action.

Dismissal Without Prejudice—Action dismissed, not on the merits, which may be re-instituted.

Dispose—The act of terminating a judicial proceeding.

Disposition—The result of a judicial proceeding by withdrawal, settlement, order, judgment, or sentence.

Disputed Claim Settlement—Settlement of a claim when there is disagreement about compensability.

Dissolution of Marriage—The effect of a judgment of dissolution of marriage is to restore the parties to the state of unmarried persons.

District Attorney—An officer of a governmental body with the duty to prosecute those accused of crimes.

Dividends—A payment that a corporation makes to its shareholders according to the number of shares outstanding.

Divorce—The legal dissolution of a marriage.

Do Not Resuscitate Order—A notation in the patient's medical record that cardiopulmonary resuscitation should not be undertaken in the event the patient suffers cardiac or respiratory arrest.

Docket—A list of cases on the court's calendar.

Domestic Corporation—In reference to a particular state, a domestic corporation is one created by, or organized under, the laws of that state.

Domestic Partnership—An ongoing relationship between two adults of the same or opposite sex who are: (i) sharing a residence; (ii) over the age of 18; (iii) emotionally interdependent; and (iv) intend to reside together indefinitely.

Domestic Relations Law—Generally refers to the body of law that governs divorce and other matrimonial actions, also known as family or matrimonial law.

Domestic Violence—Generally refers to felony or misdemeanor crimes of violence committed by a current or former spouse of the victim, by a person with whom the victim shares a child in common, by a person who is cohabitating with or has cohabited with the victim as a spouse, or by a person similarly situated to a spouse.

Domicile—Place where a person has his or her principal residence.

Double Jeopardy—Fifth Amendment provision providing that an individual shall not be subject to prosecution for the same offense more than one time.

Down Payment—A partial payment of the purchase price.

Downward Departure—Refers to a situation where a court gives a defendant a sentence that is lesser than the one provided for in the Federal Sentencing Guidelines due to certain extenuating circumstances.

Dram Shop Act—Refers to laws that impose strict liability upon the seller of intoxicating beverages when harm is caused to a third party as a result of the sale.

Due-on-Sale Clause—Provision in a mortgage or deed of trust allowing the lender to demand immediate payment of the loan balance upon sale of the property.

Due Process Rights—All rights that are of such fundamental importance as to require compliance with due process standards of fairness and justice.

Durable Power of Attorney—Also known as a "health care proxy," refers to a document naming a person to make medical decisions, in the event that the patient becomes unable to make those decisions.

Duress—Refers to the action of one person which compels another to do something he or she would not otherwise do.

Duty—The obligation, to which the law will give recognition and effect, to conform to a particular standard of conduct toward another.

E

Earned Income—Income that is gained through one's labor and services, as opposed to investment income.

Earnest Money—Deposit made by a buyer towards the down payment, in evidence of good faith, when the purchase agreement is signed.

Easement—The right to use or control the use of another's land.

Ecclesiastical Law—The body of jurisprudence administered by the ecclesiastical courts of England derived from the canon and civil law.

Ejectment—The legal action brought by one party who claims the right to possess real property being held adversely by another.

Elder Law—Laws regarding the rights of elderly people.

Elective Share—Statutory provision that a surviving spouse may choose between taking that which is provided in the spouse's will, or taking a statutorily prescribed share.

Emancipated Minor—A person who, although under the age of legal adulthood, is given certain rights of an adult under state law.

Emancipation—The surrender of care, custody and earnings of a child, as well as renunciation of parental duties.

Emergency Medical Services (EMS)—A group of governmental and private agencies that employ paramedics, first responders, and other ambulance crew to provide emergency care to persons outside of health care facilities.

Emigrant—One who leaves one country and settles in another country.

Eminent Domain—The right of the government to take private property for public use with just compensation.

Employability—The ability of an employee to meet the demands of a job and the conditions of employment.

Employee—Any individual employed by an employer.

Employee Retirement Income Security Act of 1974 (ERISA)—A federal statute that governs the administration of pension plans.

Employment Benefits—All benefits provided or made available to employees by an employer, including group life insurance, health insurance, disability insurance, sick leave, annual leave, educational benefits, and pensions, regardless of whether such benefits are provided by a practice or written policy of an employer, or through an employee benefit plan.

Employment Discrimination—Under Title VII, employment discrimination occurs when an employer denies an individual employment opportunities, or otherwise affects their terms and conditions of employment based on race, color, religion, sex, or national origin.

Encroachment—The intrusion onto another's property without right or permission.

Endangered Species—Refers to those species defined in the Endangered Species Act (16 U.S.C. 1531 et seq.).

Enforce—To put the judgment into effect by taking legal steps to bring about compliance.

Enjoin—To require a person, by writ of injunction from a court of equity, to perform, or to abstain, or desist from some act.

Enterprise—Aggregation of all establishments owned by a parent company, which may consist of a single, independent establishment or subsidiaries or other branch establishments under the same ownership and control.

Entrapment—In criminal law, refers to the use of trickery by the police to induce the defendant to commit a crime for which he or she has a predisposition to commit.

Entry—Any coming of an alien into the United States from a foreign port, or place or from an outlying possession, whether voluntarily or otherwise.

Equal Credit Opportunity Act (ECOA)—Federal law requiring creditors to make credit equally available without discrimination based on race, color, religion, national origin, age, sex, marital status, or receipt of income from public assistance programs.

Equal Employment Opportunity Commission (EEOC)—Federal agency responsible for interpreting and enforcing the employment anti-discrimination provisions under federal law, including Title VII of the Civil Rights Act of 1964.

Equitable Action—An action which may be brought for the purpose of restraining the threatened infliction of wrongs or injuries, and the prevention of threatened illegal action; case in which payment of money damages will not be adequate compensation.

Equitable Distribution—The power of the courts to equitably distribute all property legally and beneficially acquired during marriage by either spouse, whether legal title lies in their joint or individual names.

Equity—The difference between the current market value of a property and the total debt obligations against the property. On a new mortgage loan, the down payment represents the equity in the property.

Equity Financing—The provision of funds for capital or operating expenses in exchange for capital stock, stock purchase warrants and options in the business financed, without any guaranteed return, but with the opportunity to share in the company's profits.

Equity Partnership—A limited partnership arrangement for providing start-up and seed capital to businesses.

Escheat—The reversion of private property to the government under certain conditions, e.g., the absence of an heir.

Escrow—The arrangement for holding instruments, or money that is not to be released, until certain specified conditions are met.

Escrow Account—Also known as an impound account, refers to an account held by the lender to which the borrower pays monthly installments, collected as part of the monthly mortgage payment, for annual expenses such as taxes and insurance. The lender disburses escrow account funds on behalf of the borrower when they become due.

Escrow Agent—A person with fiduciary responsibility to the buyer and seller, or the borrower and lender, to ensure that the terms of the purchase/ sale or loan are carried out.

Estate—The entirety of one's property, real or personal.

Estate Tax—A tax levied on a decedent's estate in connection with the right to transfer property after death.

Estop—To stop, bar, or impede.

Estoppel—A rule of law that prevents a person from alleging or denying a fact, because of his/her own previous act.

Et al.—An abbreviation of the Latin "et alii" meaning "and others."

Et ano.—Hybrid Latin/English abbreviation meaning "and another," i.e., "and one other [party]."

Euthanasia—The act of painlessly assisting in the death of persons suffering from terminal illness or other prolonged suffering. Literally means "good death" in Greek.

Eviction—Legal mandate authorizing an enforcement officer to remove persons and their personal property from their premises.

Eviction Notice—A notice that the landlord serves on the tenant when the tenant has violated the lease or rental agreement, also known as "three-day notice." The three-day notice usually instructs the tenant to either leave the rental unit or comply with the lease or rental agreement, for example, by paying past-due rent, within the three-day period.

Evidence—A form of proof or probative matter legally presented at the trial of an issue by the acts of the parties and through witnesses, records, documents, concrete objects, etc., for the purpose of inducing belief in the minds of the court or the jury.

Ex Parte—A proceeding, order, motion, application, request, submission etc., made by or granted for the benefit of one party only.

Ex Post Facto—Latin for "after the fact."

Examination Before Trial (EBT)—A formal interrogation of parties and witnesses before trial; also referred to as a deposition.

Exchange Visitor—An alien coming temporarily to the United States as a participant in a program approved by the Secretary of State for the purpose of teaching, instructing or lecturing, studying, observing, conducting research, consulting, demonstrating special skills, or receiving training.

Excludable Alien—One who is barred from entering the United States either permanently or pending a waiver.

Exclusionary Rule—A constitutional rule of law providing that evidence procured by illegal police conduct, although otherwise admissible, will be excluded at trial.

Excuse—A matter alleged to be a reason for relief or exemption from some duty or obligation.

Execution—The performance of all acts necessary to render a written instrument complete, such as signing, sealing, acknowledging, and delivering the instrument; also refers to supplementary proceedings to enforce a judgment, which, if monetary, involves a direction to the sheriff to take the necessary steps to collect the judgment.

Executor—A person appointed by the maker of a will to carry out his or her wishes concerning the administration and distribution of his or her estate according to the terms of a will.

Executor's Deed—A deed given by an executor or other fiduciary that conveys real property.

Executory Contract—An executory contract is a contract that has not yet been fully completed or performed.

Executory Lease—A lease under which both parties to the lease have duties remaining to be performed.

Exemplification—An official transcript of a document from public records, made in a form to be used as evidence and authenticated or certified as a true copy.

Exempt—In a bankruptcy proceeding, a description of any property that a debtor may prevent creditors from recovering.

Exempt Property—Certain property owned by an individual debtor that the Bankruptcy Code or applicable state law permits the debtor to keep from unsecured creditors.

Exemption—A tax deduction granted a taxpayer who has a certain status, e.g., aged 65 or over.

Exhibit—A paper, document, or other article produced and exhibited to a court during a trial or hearing and, on being accepted, is marked for identification or admitted in evidence.

Expert Witness—A witness who has special knowledge about a certain subject, upon which he or she will testify, which knowledge is not normally possessed by the average person.

Express Warranty—A promise relating to the quality or condition of property which is usually reduced to writing.

Expunge—The authorized act of physically destroying information, in files, computers, or other depositories.

Extrajudicial—Action taken without the court's authority.

Eyewitness—A person who can testify about a matter because of his or her own presence at the time of the event.

F

Face Sheet Filing—A bankruptcy case filed either without schedules or with incomplete schedules listing few creditors and debts.

Fact Finder—In a judicial or administrative proceeding, the person, or group of persons, who has the responsibility of determining the acts relevant to decide a controversy.

Fact Finding—A process by which parties present their evidence and make their arguments to a neutral person, who issues a nonbinding report based on the findings, which usually contains a recommendation for settlement.

Fair Credit Billing Act—A federal law passed by Congress in 1975 to help customers resolve billing disputes with card issuers.

Fair Credit Reporting Act—A federal law that governs what credit bureaus can report concerning an individual consumer.

Fair Debt Collection Practices Act—A federal law that governs debt collection methods.

Fair Housing Act—Statute prohibiting housing discrimination on the basis of race, color, religion, sex, national origin, familial status, and disability.

Fair Labor Standards Act (FLSA)—Federal law governing federal wage and hour regulations.

Fair Market Value—The price at which property would be transferred between a willing buyer and willing seller, each of whom has a reasonable knowledge of all pertinent facts and is not under any compulsion to buy or sell.

False Arrest—An unlawful arrest.

False Imprisonment—Detention of an individual without justification.

False Pretense—A statutory offense whereby one obtains the property of another by making a false representation with the intent to defraud.

Family Farmer or Fisherman—An individual, individual and spouse, corporation, or partnership engaged in a farming or fishing operation that meets certain debt limits and other statutory criteria for filing a petition under chapter 12 of the Bankruptcy Code.

Family Purpose Doctrine—The doctrine that holds the owner of a family car liable in tort when it is operated negligently by another member of the family.

Fannie Mae—A common nickname for the Federal National Mortgage Association.

Featherbedding—An unfair labor practice whereby the time spent, or number of employees needed, to complete a particular task, is increased unnecessarily for the purpose of creating employment.

Federal—Of or pertaining to the Federal Government of the United States of America.

Federal Courts—The courts of the United States.

Federal Deposit Insurance Corporation (FDIC)—Independent deposit insurance agency created by Congress to maintain stability and public confidence in the nation's banking system.

Federal Employer Identification Number (FEIN)—The number assigned to a business by the Internal Revenue Service. This number is the primary identifier for employers in electronic data interchange (EDI) reporting.

Federal Home Loan Mortgage Corporation (FHLMC)—Also known as "Freddie Mac," refers to the federal agency that buys loans that are underwritten to its specific guidelines, an industry standard for residential conventional lending.

Federal Housing Administration (FHA)—A federal agency within the Department of Housing and Urban Development (HUD), which insures residential mortgage loans made by private lenders and sets standards for underwriting mortgage loans.

Federal National Mortgage Association (FNMA)—Also known as "Fannie Mae," refers to the federal agency that buys loans that are underwritten to its specific guidelines, an industry standard for residential conventional lending.

Federal Trade Commission—The Federal Trade Commission is an agency of the federal government created in 1914 for the purpose of promoting free and fair competition in interstate commerce through the prevention of general trade restraints.

Fee Simple—Type of ownership where the property owner maintains absolute ownership of real property.

Felony—A crime of a graver or more serious nature than those designated as misdemeanors.

Felony Murder—A first-degree murder charge that results when a homicide occurs during the course of certain specified felonies, such as arson and robbery.

FEPA—A state or local fair employment practices agency where many charges are first deferred for a specific time period for handling prior to being forwarded to the Equal Employment Opportunity Commission (EEOC).

FHA-Insured Loan—A fixed or adjustable rate loan insured by the U.S Department of Housing and Urban Development.

FHA Mortgage—A mortgage insured by the Federal Housing Administration.

Fiancé(e) of United States Citizen—A nonimmigrant alien coming to the United States to conclude a valid marriage with a United States citizen within ninety days of entry.

Fiduciary—A person having a legal duty, created by an undertaking, to act primarily for the benefit of another in matters connected with the undertaking.

Filing Fees—Money paid to the court clerk to file court papers and start a civil case.

Finance Charge—Any charge for an extension of credit, such as interest.

Financial Information—Refers to information identifiable to an individual that concerns the amount and conditions of an individual's assets, liabilities, or credit, including (a) Account numbers and balances; (b) Transactional information concerning an account; and (c) Codes, passwords, social security numbers, tax identification numbers, driver's license or permit numbers, state identification numbers and other information held for the purpose of account access or transaction initiation.

Financial Information Repository—Refers to a person engaged in the business of providing services to customers who have a credit, deposit, trust, stock, or other financial account or relationship with the person.

Finding—Decisions made by the court on issues of fact or law.

Fine—A financial penalty imposed upon a defendant.

First Mortgage—A mortgage that is in first lien position, taking priority over all other liens. In the case of a foreclosure, the first mortgage will be repaid before any other mortgages.

First Paper—Paper instituting an action such as a summons.

First-Time Home Buyer—A person with no ownership interest in a principal residence during the three-year period preceding the purchase of the security property.

Fiscal Year—Any twelve-month period used by a business as its fiscal accounting period. Relating to the budget year of the United States government, it begins on October 1 and ends on September 30 of the following year.

Fixed Capital—The amount of money permanently invested in a business.

Fixed Income—Income that is unchangeable.

Fixed-Period Adjustable-Rate Mortgage—An adjustable-rate mortgage (ARM) that offers a fixed rate for an initial period, typically three to ten years, and then adjusts every six months, annually, or at another specified period, for the remainder of the term.

Fixed Rate—An interest rate that is fixed for the term of the loan.

Fixed-Rate Mortgage—A mortgage with an interest rate that does not change during the entire term of the loan.

Fixture—Chattel which has become permanently and physically attached to real property, and which would not be easily removed.

Flood Certification Fee—A fee charged by independent mapping firms to identify properties located in areas designated as flood zones.

Flood Insurance—Insurance that compensates for physical damage to a property by flood. Typically not covered under standard hazard insurance.

FMLA—The Family and Medical Leave Act of 1993, Public Law 103-3 (February 5, 1993), 107 Stat. 6 (29 U.S.C. 2601 et seq.).

Forbearance—The act by the lender of refraining from taking legal action on a mortgage loan that is delinquent.

Force Majeure—A clause commonly found in construction contracts that protects the parties in the event that a part of the contract cannot be performed due to causes that are outside the control of the parties.

Forcible Entry—The entry on real property, against the possessor's will, without legal authority.

Foreclosure—Legal process by which a mortgaged property may be sold to pay off a mortgage loan that is in default.

Foreign Consul—Consular officer representing a foreign government who is located in the United States.

Foreign Corporation—In reference to a particular state, a foreign corporation is one created by or under the laws of another state, government, or country.

Foreperson—A member of a jury, usually the first juror called and sworn, or a juror elected by fellow jurors who delivers the verdict to the court.

Foreseeability—A concept used to limit the liability of a party for the consequences of his or her acts, to consequences that are within the scope of a foreseeable risk.

Forfeiture—The loss of money, property, rights, or privileges, as a punishment for some crime or misdemeanor of the party forfeiting, and as a compensation for the offense and injury committed against the one to whom they are forfeited.

Fornication—Unlawful sexual intercourse between two persons who are not married to one another.

Forum—A judicial tribunal or a place of jurisdiction. A meeting for discussion.

Forum Non Conveniens—Latin for "an inconvenient court." Refers to the right of a court to decline jurisdiction over a case when the forum would create an undue hardship on the defendants or witnesses.

Foster Children—Children who have been placed in the state's or county's legal custody because their birth parents were deemed abusive, neglectful, or otherwise unable to care for them.

Foster Parents—State or county licensed adults who provide a temporary home for children whose birth parents are unable to care for them.

Franchising—A form of business by which the owner—i.e., the franchisor—of a product, service or method obtains distribution through affiliated dealers—i.e., the franchisees—and whereby the product, method or service being marketed is usually identified by the franchisor's brand name, and the franchisee is often given exclusive access to a defined geographical area as well as assistance in organizing, training, merchandising, marketing and managing in return for a consideration.

Fraud—A false representation of a matter of fact, whether by words or by conduct, by false or misleading allegations, or by concealment of that which should have been disclosed, which deceives and is intended to deceive another, and thereby causes injury to that person.

Fraudulent Conveyance/Transfer—The transfer of property for the purpose of delaying or defrauding creditors.

Free on Board (FOB)—A commercial term that signifies a contractual agreement between a buyer and a seller to have the subject of a sale delivered to a designated place, usually either the place of shipment or the place of destination.

Freedom of Information Act (FOIA)—A federal law that requires federal agencies to disclose information in its possession that is not exempt from the law.

Freehold Estate—A real property estate with no measurable length of time or termination date.

Fresh Start—The characterization of a debtor's status after bankruptcy, i.e., free of most debts.

Full and Final Adoption—A legal adoption in which the child receives all the rights of a natural born, legitimate child.

Full Covenant and Warranty Deed—A deed conveying real property that contains a covenant that warrants title by each previous holder of warranty deeds.

Full Faith and Credit—A requirement of the U.S. Constitution that the records and judicial proceedings of one state shall have the same effect in courts of other states with the same jurisdiction.

Fully Amortized Mortgage—A mortgage in which the monthly payments are designed to retire the obligation at the end of the mortgage term.

G

Gag Order—An order imposed by the court restricting comment about a case.

Garnish—To attach a portion of the wages or other property of a debtor to secure repayment of the debt.

Garnishee—A person who receives notice to hold the assets of another, which are in his or her possession, until such time as a court orders the disposition of the property.

General Damages—General damages are those damages directly referable to the breach or tortious act and which can be readily proven to have been sustained, and for which the injured party should be compensated as a matter of right.

General Partner—A partner who participates fully in the profits, losses and management of the partnership, and who is personally liable for its debts.

General Partnership—A type of partnership in which all of the partners share the profits and losses as well as the management fully, though their capital contributions may vary.

Gerrymander—The process of creating an unusually shaped civil division within an area for an improper purpose.

Gift Tax—A tax assessed against the transferor of a gift of property, based upon the fair market value of the property on the date transferred.

Good Cause—A sufficient reason.

Good Faith Estimate—Written estimate of the settlement costs the borrower will likely have to pay at closing. Under the Real Estate Settlement Procedures Act (RESPA), the lender is required to provide this disclosure to the borrower within three days of receiving a loan application.

Grace Period—In contract law, a period specified in a contract that is beyond the due date but during which time, payment will be accepted without penalty. In the case of a loan, the period of time during which a loan payment may be made after its due date without incurring a late penalty. The grace period is specified as part of the terms of the loan in the Note.

Graft—The fraudulent receipt of public money by a public official.

Grand Jury—A group of people summoned to court to investigate a crime and hand down an indictment if sufficient evidence is presented to hold the accused for trial.

Grantee—One who receives a conveyance of real property by deed.

Grantor—One who conveys real property by deed.

Green Card—A wallet-sized card showing that the person is a lawful permanent resident of the United States. It is also known as a permanent resident card (PRC), an alien registration receipt card and I-551. It was formerly green in color.

Gross Income—Total income before taxes or expenses are deducted.

Gross Negligence—The intentional failure to meet the required standard of care in reckless disregard of the consequences to another.

Guaranteed Loan—A loan made and serviced by a lending institution under agreement that a governmental agency will purchase the guaranteed portion if the borrower defaults.

Guarantor—One who makes a guaranty.

Guaranty—An agreement to perform the duty of another person if that person reneges on a promise contained in an underlying agreement.

Guardian—A person who is entrusted with the management of the property and/or of a person who is incapable, due to age or incapacity, to administer their own affairs.

Guardian Ad Litem—Latin for "guardian at law." Refers to the person appointed by a court to represent a minor or incompetent for purpose of a court proceeding.

Guardian of the Estate—A guardian who possesses any or all powers and rights with regard to the property of the ward.

Guardian of the Person—A person who is responsible for and who advocates for the health, well-being, and personal needs of the ward.

Guardian of the Person and Estate—A person who acts in both capacities for a ward.

H

Habeas Corpus—Latin for "You have the body." Refers to a procedure brought by writ to determine the legality of an individual's custody.

Habendum—A clause in a deed naming the grantee and defining the estate to be granted.

Habitability—Refers to premises in which the conditions are safe, healthy and fit for occupation.

Halfway House—A residence where individuals who have been released from a very structured environment, such as a mental institution or prison, are supervised and taught to readjust to society.

Hallucination—The perception by one's senses of something that does not exist in reality.

Hallucinogens—Natural and man-made drugs which affect the mind, causing distortions in physical senses and mental reactions.

Harmless Error—An error committed by a lower court proceeding that does not substantially violate an appellant's rights to an extent that the lower court proceeding should be modified or overturned.

Hazard Insurance—Protects the insured against loss due to fire or other natural disaster in exchange for a premium paid to the insurer.

Head Note—The summary of the issues contained in a reported case, which appears at the beginning of the case note.

Health Care Agent—The person named in an advance directive, or as permitted under state law, to make health care decisions on behalf of a person who is no longer able to make medical decisions.

Health Care Decision—A decision made by an individual or the individual's agent, guardian, or surrogate, regarding the individual's health care, including: (1) selection and discharge of health-care providers and institutions; (2) approval or disapproval of diagnostic tests, surgical procedures, programs of medication, and orders not to resuscitate; and (3) directions to provide, withhold, or withdraw artificial nutrition and hydration, and all other forms of health care.

Health Care Institution—An institution, facility, or agency licensed, certified, or otherwise authorized or permitted by law to provide health care in the ordinary course of business.

Health Care Provider—A person who is licensed, certified, registered, or otherwise authorized by law to administer or provide health care in the ordinary course of business, or in the practice of a profession.

Health Care Proxy—Any person lawfully designated to act on behalf of an individual.

Health Insurance Portability and Accountability Act (HIPAA)— A federal law enacted in 1996, designated to improve availability and portability of health coverage and the efficiency of the health care system by standardizing the electronic exchange of health information and protecting the security and privacy of member-identifiable health information.

Hearing—A proceeding during which evidence is taken for the purpose of determining the facts of a dispute and reaching a decision.

Hearsay Rule—The evidence rule that declares any statement, other than that by a witness who is testifying at the hearing, is not admissible as evidence to prove the truth of the matter asserted, unless it falls under an exception to the rule.

Heir—An individual who, by law, inherits an estate of an ancestor who dies without a will.

Hereditament—Anything that can be inherited.

Hereditary Succession—The passing of title to an estate according to the laws of descent.

HIPAA—See **Health Insurance Portability and Accountability Act (HIPAA)**.

Holder in Due Course—One who has taken an instrument, complete and regular on its face, before it was overdue, in good faith and for value, without notice of any infirmity in the instrument or defect in the title of the person negotiating.

Holding Deposit—A deposit that a tenant gives to a landlord to hold a rental unit until the tenant pays the first month's rent and the security deposit.

Homestead—The house, outbuilding, and land owned and used as a dwelling by the head of the family.

Homicide—The killing of a human being by another human being.

Hornbook—A book that contains the fundamental principles of a particular subject.

Hostile Possession—The actual possession of real property without the permission of the legal owner, with a claim of implied ownership by the possessor.

Hostile Work Environment—A working environment that both a reasonable person would find hostile or abusive, and one that the particular person who is the object of the harassment perceives to be hostile or abusive. In a sexual harassment claim, a hostile work environment is one in which the victim is subjected to unwelcome and severe or pervasive repeated sexual comments, innuendoes, touching, or other conduct of a sexual nature which creates an intimidating or offensive place for employees to work.

Housing and Urban Development (HUD)—A federal government agency established to implement federal housing and community development programs; oversees the Federal Housing Administration.

HUD-1 Uniform Settlement Statement—A standard form that itemizes the closing costs associated with purchasing a home or refinancing a loan.

Hung Jury—A jury that cannot render a verdict because its members cannot reconcile their differences to a necessary standard, e.g., unanimity, substantial majority.

Hypothetical Question—A question that assumes certain facts and calls for an opinion based on those assumptions.

I

Ignorance—Lack of knowledge.

Ignorantia Legis Non Excusat—Latin for "Ignorance of the law is no excuse." Although an individual may not think an act is illegal, the act is still punishable.

Illegal—Against the law.

Illegitimacy—A child who is born at a time when his parents are not married to each other.

Illegitimate—Illegal or improper. Also used to describe the status of children born out of wedlock.

Illusory Promise—A promise that is unenforceable because its conditions are so indefinite.

Immaterial—Evidence that is not offered to prove a material issue.

Immigrant—An alien who enters the United States with the intent of remaining for an indefinite period of time.

Immigrant Visa—A visa for a person who plans to live indefinitely and permanently in the United States.

Immigration—The act of permanently moving one's residence from their original country into a foreign country.

Immigration Act of 1990—Public Law 101-649 (Act of November 29, 1990), which increased the limits on legal immigration to the United States, revised all grounds for exclusion and deportation, authorized temporary protected status to aliens of designated countries, revised and established new nonimmigrant admission categories, revised and extended the Visa Waiver Pilot Program, and revised naturalization authority and requirements.

Immigration and Nationality Act (INA)—American immigration law. The Immigration and Nationality Act, or INA, was created in 1952, Public Law No. 82-414. The INA has been amended many times over the years, but is still the basic body of immigration law.

Immigration and Naturalization Service (INS)—A branch of the Department of Justice that formerly existed and had responsibility for immigration and naturalization. The INS was renamed and became part of the Department of Homeland Security (DHS) on March 1, 2003.

Immigration Judge—An attorney appointed by the Attorney General to act as an administrative judge within the Executive Office for Immigration Review.

Immigration Marriage Fraud Amendments of 1986—Public Law 99-639 (Act of 11/10/86), which was passed in order to deter immigration-related marriage fraud.

Immigration Reform and Control Act (IRCA) of 1986—Public Law 99-603 (Act of 11/6/86), which was passed in order to control and deter illegal immigration to the United States.

Immunity—A benefit of exemption from a duty or penalty.

Impairment—The loss, or loss of use, of any body part, system, or function.

Impaneling—Selecting and swearing in a panel of jurors for duty.

Impeach—A showing by means of evidence that the testimony of a witness was unworthy of belief. Also refers to the process of charging a public official with a wrong while still holding office.

Impleader—The process of bringing a third potentially liable party into a pending suit.

Implied Consent—Consent that is manifested by signs, actions or facts, or by inaction or silence, which raises a presumption that consent has been given.

Implied Warranty—A warranty relating to the quality or condition of property that is implied by law to exist.

Implied Warranty of Habitability—A legal rule that requires landlords to maintain their rental units in a condition fit for human beings to live in. In addition, a rental unit must substantially comply with building and housing code standards that materially affect tenants' health and safety.

Impossibility—Impossibility is a defense to breach of contract and arises when performance is impossible due to the destruction of the subject matter of the contract or the death of a person necessary for performance.

Impound—To place property in the custody of an official.

Impound Account—Also known as an escrow account, refers to an account held by the lender to which the borrower pays monthly installments, collected as part of the monthly mortgage payment, for annual expenses such as taxes and insurance. The lender disburses impound account funds on behalf of the borrower when they become due.

Imprisonment—The confinement of an individual, usually as punishment for a crime.

Improvement—The development of land or structures to increase the property value.

In Camera—Latin for "in chambers." Refers to proceedings held in the privacy of a judge's chambers.

In Forma Pauperis—Latin for "in the manner of a pauper." It refers to the right of a party to proceed with a lawsuit without costs or certain formalities.

In Loco Parentis—Latin for "in the place of a parent." Refers to an individual who assumes parental obligations and status without a formal, legal adoption.

In Re—Latin for "in the matter of."

In Rem—Latin for "against the thing." Refers to actions that are against property, and concerned with the disposition of that property, rather than against the person.

Inadmissible Evidence—evidence or testimony that does not meet the state or federal court rules that govern that types of evidence that can be presented in court to a judge or a jury and is therefore excluded from consideration.

Incapacity—Incapacity is a defense to breach of contract that refers to a lack of legal, physical, or intellectual power to enter into a contract.

Incest—The crime of sexual intercourse or cohabitation between a man and woman who are related to each other within the degrees wherein marriage is prohibited by law.

Inchoate—That which is not yet completed or finished.

Incompetency—Lack of legal qualification or fitness to discharge a legally required duty or to handle one's own affairs; also refers to matters not admissible in evidence.

Incorporation—To form a corporation by following established legal procedures.

Indemnification Clause—An indemnification clause in a contract refers to the agreement by one party to secure the other party against loss or damage which may occur in the future, in connection with performance of the contract.

Indemnify—To hold another harmless for loss or damage which has already occurred, or which may occur in the future.

Indemnity—Amount paid as compensation under an indemnity agreement.

Independent Contractor—An individual who contracts to perform services for others without qualifying legally as an employee.

Index—A published rate used by lenders that serves as the basis for determining interest rate changes on adjustable rate mortgage loans.

Indictment—A formal written accusation of criminal charges submitted to a grand jury for investigation and endorsement.

Indigent—A person who is financially destitute.

Indispensable Party—A party without whom a lawsuit may not proceed unless he or she is joined, due to that party's interest in the matter.

Individual Retirement Account (IRA)—A retirement plan for individuals who are not eligible for a pension or profit-sharing plan.

Individuals with Disabilities Education Act (IDEA)—A statute requiring public schools to provide a free public education to disabled children in the least restrictive environment appropriate for the child's needs.

Industrial Revenue Bond (IRB)—A tax-exempt bond issued by a state or local government agency to finance industrial or commercial projects that serve a public good. The bond usually is not backed by the full faith and credit of the government that issues it, but is repaid solely from the revenues of the project and requires a private sector commitment for repayment.

Infancy—The state of a person who is under the age of legal majority.

Infancy Presumption—At common law, the conclusive presumption that children under the age of seven were without criminal capacity.

Infant's Compromise—A civil proceeding or motion for obtaining court approval of the settlement of an infant's claim.

Inference—A reasoned deduction based on the given facts.

Information—A written accusation of a crime submitted by the prosecutor to inform the accused and the court of the charges, and the facts of the crime.

Informed Consent—The requirement that a patient be apprised of the nature and risks of a medical procedure before the physician can validly claim exemption from liability for battery, or from responsibility for medical complications.

Informer—An individual who gives information concerning criminal activities to governmental authorities on a confidential basis.

Inhalants—Chemicals which emit fumes or vapors which, when inhaled, produce symptoms similar to intoxication.

Inherit—To take as an heir at law by descent rather than by will.

Inheritance—Property inherited by heirs according to the laws of descent and distribution.

Inheritance Tax—A tax levied on heirs in connection with the right to receive property from a decedent's estate.

Initial Rate—The rate charged during the first interval of an Adjustable Rate Mortgage (ARM).

Injunction—A judicial remedy either requiring a party to perform an act, or restricting a party from continuing a particular act.

Injury—Any damage done to another's person, rights, reputation, or property.

Inquest—A proceeding which usually is a limited non-jury trial for the purpose of fixing the amount of damages where the plaintiff or defendant alone introduces testimony.

Insolvency—The inability of a borrower to meet financial obligations as they mature, or having insufficient assets to pay legal debts.

Installment Contract—An installment contract is one in which the obligation, such as the payment of money, is divided into a series of successive performances over a period of time.

Instruction—Directions concerning the applicable law of a case, which are given to the jury by the judge, prior to their deliberation.

Insufficient Evidence—The judicial decision that the evidence submitted to prove a case does not meet the degree necessary to go forward with the action.

Insurance—A contingency agreement, supported by consideration, whereby the insured receives a benefit, e.g., money, in the event the contingency occurs.

Insurer Medical Examination (IME)—Also referred to as an independent medical examination. A medical examination of an injured worker by a physician other than the worker's attending physician, at the request of the insurer.

Intellectual Property—The ownership of ideas and control over the tangible or virtual representation of those ideas.

Intentional Tort—A tort or wrong perpetrated by one who intends to do that which the law has declared wrong, as contrasted with negligence in which the tortfeasor fails to exercise that degree of care in doing what is otherwise permissible.

Inter Alia—Among other things.

Inter Vivos—Latin for "between the living." Refers to transactions made during the lifetime of the parties.

Interest—An amount of money paid by a borrower to a lender for the use of the lender's money.

Interest Rate—The percentage of a sum of money charged for its use.

Interest Rate Cap—Consumer safeguards that limit the amount the interest rate on an adjustable rate mortgage loan can change in an adjustment interval and/or over the life of the loan.

Interested Parties—Heirs, devises, children, spouses, creditors, beneficiaries and any others having a right in, or claims against, the estate of a ward or protected person that may be affected by guardianship proceedings.

Interim Order—An order that is issued temporarily until a certain event takes place, or a final order is issued.

Interlocutory Order—An order that determines an issue during the course of litigation, but does not dispose of the case.

International Adoption—The adoption of a child who is a citizen of one country by adoptive parents who are citizens of a different country.

International Law—The law that governs the relationship among the nations.

Interpleader—Action by which one having possession of an article or fund claimed by two parties may compel them to litigate the title between themselves, instead of with the one having possession.

Interpreter—A person sworn, at a judicial proceeding, to translate oral or written language.

Interrogatories—A pretrial discovery method whereby written questions are served by one party to the action upon the other, who must reply, in writing, under oath.

Interstate—A region comprised of multiple states.

Intervention—A proceeding permitting an individual to intervene in a pending action when that individual has an interest that may be affected by the litigation.

Intestate—The state of dying without having executed a valid will.

Intestate Succession—The manner of disposing of property according to the laws of descent and distribution when the decedent died without leaving a valid will.

Intrastate—A region within a single state.

Investigator (INS)—Law enforcement official responsible for detecting illegal aliens and taking them into custody.

Invitee—One who enters another's property by invitation.

Involuntary Petition—A petition filed by an individual's creditors attempting to force him or her into bankruptcy.

Involuntary Servitude—A condition of servitude induced by means of any scheme, plan, or pattern intended to cause a person to believe that, if the person did not enter into or continue in such condition, that person or another person would suffer serious harm or physical restraint; or (b) the abuse or threatened abuse of the legal process.

Issue Preclusion—The doctrine which states that an issue which has already been decided cannot be relitigated.

J

Jail—Place of confinement where a person in custody of the government awaits trial or serves a sentence after conviction.

Jailhouse Lawyer—An inmate who gains knowledge of the law through self-study, and assists fellow inmates in preparation of appeals, although he or she is not licensed to practice law.

Joinder—The unification of multiple causes of action or parties in a single lawsuit.

Joint and Several—The rights and liabilities shared among a group of people individually and collectively.

Joint Liability—Liability shared among two or more people, each of whom is liable for the full debt.

Joint Petition—One bankruptcy petition filed by a husband and wife together.

Joint Tenancy—The ownership of property by two or more persons who each have an undivided interest in the whole property, with the right of survivorship, whereby upon the death of one joint tenant, the remaining joint tenants assume ownership.

Joint Trial—Two or more actions involving a common question of law or fact which may be joined by court order for trial but remain separate and distinct, and may result in one or more verdicts and judgments.

Jones Act—The federal statute permitting a seaman, or a representative, the right to sue for personal injuries suffered in the course of the seaman's employment.

Judge—The individual who presides over a court, and whose function it is to determine controversies.

Judgment—A judgment is a final determination by a court of law concerning the rights of the parties to a lawsuit.

Judgment by Confession—The act of debtors permitting judgment to be entered against them for a given sum with a statement to that effect, without the institution of legal proceedings.

Judgment Creditor—A creditor who has obtained a judgment against a debtor, which judgment may be enforced to obtain payment of the amount due.

Judgment Debtor—An individual who owes a sum of money, and against whom a judgment has been awarded for that debt.

Judgment of Divorce—A document signed by the court granting the divorce.

Judgment Proof—Refers to the status of an individual who does not have the financial resources or assets necessary to satisfy a judgment.

Judgment Roll—A record of a judgment with the supporting papers.

Judicial Notice—The doctrine whereby the court takes note of certain facts that are indisputable, thereby relieving one party of the burden of proving the fact.

Jumbo Loan—A mortgage larger than the $240,000 limit set by the Federal National Mortgage Association and the Federal Home Loan Mortgage Corporation.

Junior Mortgage—A mortgage subordinate to the claim of a prior lien or mortgage. In the case of a foreclosure, a senior mortgage or lien will be paid first.

Juris Doctor (J.D.)—The degree awarded an individual who completes legal studies.

Jurisdiction—The geographical, subject matter, and monetary limitations of a court to hear and determine a case.

Jurisdictional Limit—The maximum monetary amount that may be awarded by a small claims court.

Jurisprudence—The study of legal systems and the law.

Jury—A group of individuals summoned to decide the facts in issue in a lawsuit.

Jury Trial—A trial during which the evidence is presented to a jury so that they can determine the issues of fact, and render a verdict based upon the law as it applies to their findings of fact.

Justification—A just, lawful excuse, or reason for an act, or failing to act.

Juvenile Court—A court that has special jurisdiction, of a parental nature, over delinquent, dependent, and neglected children.

Juvenile Delinquent—An infant of not more than a specified age who has violated criminal laws or has engaged in disobedient, indecent or immoral conduct, and is in need of treatment, rehabilitation, or supervision.

K

Kangaroo Court—A court that operates without legal authority and in disregard of the rights normally afforded individuals.

Kickback—The practice of a provider of goods or services to pay the purchaser part of the purchase price as an inducement to enter into the transaction.

Kidnapping—The illegal taking of a person against his or her will.

L

Labor Certificate—The document issued by the U.S. Department of Labor to an alien certifying that U.S. workers are not adversely affected by the alien's employment.

Labor Certification—Requirement for U.S. employers seeking to employ certain persons whose immigration to the United States is based on job skills, or nonimmigrant temporary workers coming to perform services for which qualified authorized workers are unavailable in the United States.

Labor Organization—An association of workers for the purpose of bargaining the terms and conditions of employment on behalf of labor and management.

Laches—An undue lapse of time in enforcing a cause of action, which as an equitable defense may bar the plaintiff from pursuing the claim.

Larceny—The unlawful taking of the property of another, without his or her consent, with the intention of converting it to one's own use.

Last Clear Chance—The doctrine under which a defendant may be held liable for damages to a plaintiff guilty of contributory negligence where the defendant could have avoided injuring the plaintiff by exercising due care.

Late Charge—Penalty paid by a borrower when a payment is made after the due date.

Law Enforcement—Generally refers to public agencies charged with policing functions, including any of their component bureaus.

Lawful Permanent Resident (LPR)—A person who has immigrated legally but is not an American citizen. Also referred to as a legal permanent resident, a green card holder, a permanent resident alien, a legal permanent resident alien (LPRA), and resident alien permit holder.

Lay Witness—Any witness not testifying as an expert witness.

Leading Question—A question which, by its wording, suggests a response to the witness.

Lease—A contract between an owner—i.e., a lessor—and a tenant—i.e., a lessee—stating the conditions under which the tenant may occupy or use the property.

Leave of Court—Permission obtained from the court to take some action that would be otherwise impermissible.

Legacy—A gift of personal property by will.

Legal Aid—A national organization established to provide legal services to those who are unable to afford private representation.

Legal Capacity—Referring to the legal capacity to sue, it is the requirement that a person bringing the lawsuit have a sound mind, be of lawful age, and be under no restraint or legal disability.

Legal Custody—The assumption of responsibility for a minor by an adult under the laws of the state and under the order or approval of a court of law or other appropriate government entity.

Legal Description—A means of identifying the exact boundaries of land.

Legal Representative—Refers to a representative payee, a guardian or conservator acting for a ward or conservatee, a trustee or custodian of a trust or custodianship of which the ward or conservatee is a beneficiary, or an agent designated under a power of attorney, whether for health care or property, in which the ward or conservatee is identified as the principal.

Legalized Aliens—Certain illegal aliens who were eligible to apply for temporary resident status under the legalization provision of the Immigration Reform and Control Act of 1986.

Legatee—One who takes a legacy.

Legislation—Laws enacted by state or federal representatives.

Lemon Laws—Refers to state legislation affording certain remedies to the purchasers of new or used vehicles which are discovered to have recurrent repair problems which are not able to be resolved by the manufacturer or dealer of the vehicle.

Lender—A bank, mortgage company, or mortgage broker offering to loan money.

Lending Institution—Any institution, including a commercial bank, savings and loan association, commercial finance company, or other lender qualified to participate in the making of loans.

Letter of Conservatorship—An official letter that serves as written evidence of the appointment of a conservator and the authority of the conservator to act for the conservatee.

Letter of Guardianship—An official letter that serves as written evidence of the appointment of a guardian and the authority of the guardian to act for the ward.

Letter of Intent—A non-binding writing intended to set forth the intentions between parties in anticipation of a formal, binding contract.

Letters of Administration—A formal document issued by a court that authorizes a person to act as an administrator for the estate of a deceased person.

Levy—To seize property in order to satisfy a judgment.

Liability—Liability refers to one's obligation to do or refrain from doing something, such as the payment of a debt.

Liability on Account—Legal responsibility to repay debt.

Libel—The false and malicious publication, in printed form, for the purpose of defaming another.

Liber—A book used for keeping a record of specific documents or events having legal effect.

LIBOR (London Interbank Offered Rate)—The interest rate charged among banks in the foreign market for short-term loans to one another, which is a common index for adjustable rate loans.

License—A privilege to perform some act upon the land of another without possessing any estate therein.

Licensee—A licensee upon one's land is one who is privileged to enter or remain on the land only by virtue of the landowner's consent.

Lien—A legal claim by one person on the property of another as security for payment of a debt.

LIFE Act—Refers to the Legal Immigration Family Equity (LIFE) Act, which allows foreign spouses of American citizens, the children of those foreign spouses, and spouses and children of certain lawful permanent residents (LPR) to come to the United States to complete the processing for their permanent residence.

Life Estate—An estate in land held during the term of a specified person's life.

Life Expectancy—The period of time a person is statistically expected to live, based on such factors as their present age and sex.

Life Insurance—A contract between an insured and an insurer whereby the insurer promises to pay a sum of money upon the death of the insured to his or her designated beneficiary, in return for the periodic payment of money, known as a premium.

Life-Sustaining Treatment—Any medical treatment, procedure, or intervention that, in the judgment of the attending physician, when applied to the patient, would serve only to prolong the dying process where the patient has a terminal illness or injury, or would serve only to maintain the patient in a condition of permanent unconsciousness.

Limited Conservator—One appointed by the court to assist in managing the financial resources of a partially disabled person, and one whose powers and duties have been specifically listed by court order.

Limited Guardian—A guardian with fewer than all the powers and duties of a full guardian, and whose powers and duties have been specifically listed by court order.

Limited Liability—An organization has the characteristic of limited liability if under local law there is no member who is personally liable for the organization's debts.

Limited Liability Company (LLC)—A hybrid business formation with certain advantageous features of both a partnership (e.g., pass through income) and a corporation (e.g., limited liability).

Limited Partner—A partner whose participation in the profits of the business is limited by agreement and who is not liable for the debts of the partnership beyond his or her capital contribution.

Limited Partnership—A type of partnership comprised of one or more general partners who manage the business and who are personally liable for partnership debts, and one or more limited partners who contribute capital and share in profits but who take no part in running the business and incur no liability with respect to partnership obligations beyond contribution.

Lineup—A police procedure whereby a suspect is placed in line with other persons of similar description so that a witness to the crime may attempt an identification.

Liquidated Claim—In a bankruptcy proceeding, a creditor's claim for a fixed amount of money.

Liquidated Damages—An amount stipulated in a contract as a reasonable estimate of damages to be paid in the event the contract is breached.

Liquidation—A sale of a debtor's property with the proceeds to be used for the benefit of creditors.

Liquidation Value—The net value realizable in the sale—ordinarily a forced sale—of a business or a particular asset.

Listing Agreement—A contract between the seller of property and the broker providing that the broker will receive a commission upon finding a buyer who is ready, willing, and able to purchase the seller's property.

Litigant—Party to a legal action.

Litigation—The practice of taking legal action through the judicial process.

Living Trust—A trust that is operated during the life of the creator of the trust.

Living Will—A declaration that states an individual's wishes concerning the use of extraordinary life support systems.

Loan—The grant of a temporary use of money by a lender to be repaid later, usually with interest.

Loan Agreement—Agreement to be executed by borrower, containing pertinent terms, conditions, covenants and restrictions.

Loan Application—An initial statement of personal and financial information required to apply for a loan.

Loan Application Fee—Fee charged by a lender to cover the initial costs of processing a loan application. The fee may include the cost of obtaining a property appraisal, a credit report, and a lock-in fee or other closing costs incurred during the process, or the fee may be in addition to these charges.

Loan Origination Fee—Fee charged by a lender to cover administrative costs of processing a loan.

Loan Principal—The loan principal is the amount of the debt not including interest or any other additions.

Loan-to-Value Ratio (LTV)—The percentage of the mortgage loan amount to the appraised value (or the sales price, whichever is less) of the property.

Lock or Lock-In—A mortgage lender's guarantee of an interest rate for a set period of time. The time period is usually that between loan application approval and loan closing. The lock-in protects the borrower against rate increases during that time.

Lockout—When a landlord locks a tenant out of the rental unit with the intent of terminating the tenancy. Lockouts, and all other self-help eviction remedies, are illegal.

Long Arm Statutes—Laws enacted to permit local courts jurisdiction over nonresident defendants when the cause of action occurs within their locality, and affects the rights of local citizens.

Long-Term Care—The services provided at home or in an institutionalized setting to older persons who require medical or personal care for an extended period of time.

Long-Term Care Ombudsman—An independent advocate for nursing home residents.

Lump Sum—Payment of all or any part of permanent partial disability award in one payment.

M

Magnuson-Moss Warranty Act—A federal law governing the placement and content of written warranties on consumer products.

Maintain Status—To follow the requirements of the visa status and comply with any limitations on duration of stay.

Maintenance—The furnishing by one person to another the means of living, or food, clothing, shelter, etc., particularly where the legal relations of the parties is such that one is bound to support the other, as between parent and child, or between spouses.

Maker—As used in commercial law, the individual who executes a note.

Malfeasance—The commission of an illegal or wrongful act.

Malice—A state of mind that accompanies the intentional commission of a wrongful act.

Malicious Prosecution—A cause of action against those who prosecuted unsuccessful civil or criminal actions with malicious intent.

Malpractice—The improper performance of professional responsibilities.

Mann Act—A federal statute prohibiting the transportation of a female across state lines for the purpose of prostitution.

Manslaughter—The unlawful taking of another's life without malice aforethought.

Margin—A specified percentage that is added to a chosen financial index to determine the interest rate at the time of adjustment for adjustable rate mortgage loans.

Marital Assets—Any property, regardless of the named owner, that is acquired by either spouse, from the date of marriage to the commencement of the divorce action, e.g., a house, car, IRA, joint bank account, pension, or annuity.

Martial Law—The control of the military over civilians during a state of extreme emergency, such as war.

Material Breach—A material breach refers to a substantial breach of contract that excuses further performance by the innocent party and gives rise to an action for breach of contract by the injured party.

Material Witness—A person whose testimony on some issue has been judicially determined as relevant and substantial.

Maturity Date—The date upon which a creditor is designated to receive payment of a debt, such as payment of the principal value of a bond to a bondholder by the issuing company or governmental entity.

Maturity Extensions—Extensions of payment beyond the original period established for repayment of a loan.

Means of Identification—As it pertains to identity theft, refers to any name or number that may be used, alone or in conjunction with any other information, to identify a specific individual, including a current or former name of the person, telephone number, an electronic address, or identifier of the individual or a member of his or her family, including the ancestor of the person; information relating to a change in name, address, telephone number, or electronic address or identifier of the individual or his or her family; a social security, driver's license, or tax identification number of the individual or a member of his or her family; and other information that could be used to identify the person, including unique biometric data.

Means Test—Test applied to determine whether an individual debtor's chapter 7 filing is presumed to be an abuse of the Bankruptcy Code requiring dismissal, or conversion of the case to a chapter 13 case.

Mechanic's Lien—A claim created by law for the purpose of securing a priority of payment of the price of work performed and materials furnished.

Mediation—The act of a third person in intermediating between two contending parties with a view to persuading them to adjust or settle their dispute but without the authority to make a binding decision.

Mediation and Conciliation Service—An independent department of the federal government charged with trying to settle labor disputes by conciliation and mediation.

Mediation/Arbitration—Combination of mediation and arbitration that utilizes a neutral selected to serve as both mediator and arbitrator in a dispute.

Mediator—One who interposes between parties at variance for the purpose of reconciling them.

Medicaid—A federal program, financed by federal, state, and local governments, intended to provide access to health care services for the poor.

Medical Malpractice—The failure of a physician to exercise that degree of skill and learning commonly applied under all the circumstances in the community by the average prudent reputable professional in the same field.

Medical Provider—A hospital, medical clinic, or other vendor of medical services.

Medicare—The program governed by the Social Security Administration to provide medical and hospital coverage to the aged or disabled.

Medicare Part A—Medicare coverage for hospitalization, extended care and nursing home care.

Medicare Part B—Medicare coverage for outpatient services, subject to a monthly premium.

Mens Rea—Latin for "a guilty mind."

Mental Abuse—The intentional infliction of anguish, degradation, fear, or distress through verbal or nonverbal acts.

Mental Cruelty—As used in divorce law, a course of cruel conduct towards one's spouse which so endangers their mental and physical health that it renders the marriage unbearable.

Meretricious—Of or relating to an unlawful sexual connection.

Merger—A combination of two or more corporations wherein the dominant unit absorbs the passive ones, and the former continuing operation usually under the same name.

Merger Clause—A merger clause is a provision in a contract that states that the written terms of the agreement may not be varied by prior or oral agreements because all such agreements are said to have merged into the writing.

Merit Resolution—A charge with an outcome favorable to the charging parties and/or a charge with meritorious allegations. A merit resolution may include negotiated settlements, withdrawals with benefits, successful conciliations, and unsuccessful conciliations.

Migrant—A person who leaves his or her country of origin to seek residence in another country.

Military Calendar—To hold in suspense an action that cannot reasonably be tried because a party or witness is in the military service.

Minitrial—A confidential, nonbinding exchange of information intended to facilitate settlement.

Minor—A person who has not yet reached the age of legal competence, which is designated as 18 in most states.

Minute Book—A court clerk's journal of courtroom proceedings.

Minutes—A record of court proceedings kept by noting significant events.

Miranda Rule—The law requiring that a person receive certain warnings concerning the privilege against self-incrimination, prior to custodial interrogation, as set forth in the landmark case of *Miranda v. Arizona.*

Misdemeanor—Criminal offenses that are less serious than felonies and carry lesser penalties.

Misfeasance—The commission of a lawful act in a wrongful manner.

Mistrial—A trial that is terminated prior to the return of a verdict, such as occurs when the jury is unable to reach a verdict.

Mitigating Circumstances—Circumstances that may reduce the penalty connected with the offense.

Mitigation of Damages—The requirement that a person damaged due to another's acts, such as a breach of contract, must act reasonably to avoid or limit their losses, or risk denial of recovery for damages that could have been avoided.

Modus Operandi—Latin for "the manner of operation." Refers to the characteristic method used by a criminal in carrying out his or her actions.

Monthly Income—In a bankruptcy proceeding, the average monthly income received by the debtor over the six calendar months before commencement of the bankruptcy case.

Moot—Without legal significance.

Mortgage—A written instrument, duly executed and delivered, that creates a lien upon real estate as security for the payment of a specific debt.

Mortgage Banker—An individual or company that originates and/or services mortgage loans.

Mortgage Broker—An individual or company that arranges financing for borrowers.

Mortgage Loan—A loan for which real estate serves as collateral to provide for repayment in case of default.

Mortgage Note—Legal document obligating a borrower to repay a loan at a stated interest rate during a specified period of time. The agreement is secured by a mortgage, deed of trust, or other security instrument.

Mortgagee—The lender in a mortgage loan transaction.

Mortgagor—The borrower in a mortgage loan transaction.

Motion—An application to the court requesting an order or ruling in favor of the applicant.

Motion to Lift the Automatic Stay—In a bankruptcy proceeding, a request by a creditor to allow the creditor to take action against the debtor or the debtor's property that would otherwise be prohibited by the automatic stay.

Motion to Quash Service of Summons—In landlord-tenant law, a legal response that a tenant can file in an unlawful detainer lawsuit if the tenant believes that the landlord did not properly serve the summons and complaint.

Movant—The party who initiates a motion.

Multiple Listing Service (MLS)—A cooperative listing arrangement whereby participating brokers enter property listings, which are thereby distributed to other brokers to assist in selling the listed properties.

Municipal Corporation—Generally, refers to incorporated cities, towns, and villages.

Municipal Court—A city court that administers the law within the city.

Municipal Ordinance—The violation of a city law.

Mutual Agreement—Mutual agreement refers to the meeting of the minds of the parties to a contract concerning the subject matter of the contract.

N

Narcotics—Generic term for any drug that dulls the senses or induces sleep and which commonly becomes addictive after prolonged use.

National—Of a nationwide character, including the state, local, and tribal aspects of governance and policy.

National Association of Realtors (NAR)—The largest membership organization of persons representing the real estate industry.

National Labor Relations Act—A federal statute known as the Wagner Act of 1935 and amended by the Taft-Hartley Act of 1947, which established the National Labor Relations Board to regulate the relations between employers and employees.

National Labor Relations Board—An independent agency created by the National Labor Relations Act of 1935 (Wagner Act), as amended by the acts of 1947 (Taft-Hartley Act) and 1959 (Landrum-Griffin Act), established to regulate the relations between employers and employees.

National Mediation Board—Organization created by Congress in 1934, amending the Railway Labor Act, for the purpose of mediating disputes over wages, hours, and working conditions that arise between rail and air carriers, and their employees.

National of the United States—A citizen of the United States and any other person who, although not a citizen, owes permanent allegiance to the United States.

Native—A person born in a particular country is a native of that country.

Natural Person—A human being as opposed to an artificial "person" such as a corporation.

Naturalization—A citizen who acquires nationality of a country after birth. That is, the person did not become a citizen by birth, but by a legal procedure.

Naturalization Application—The form used by a lawful permanent resident to apply for U.S. citizenship.

Naturalization Examiner—Governmental official who conducts investigations concerning alien eligibility for citizenship in the United States.

Naturalized Citizen—A foreign-born person who has been granted U.S. citizenship.

Negative Amortization—A loan payment schedule in which the outstanding principal balance of a loan goes up rather than down because the payments do not cover the full amount of interest due. The monthly shortfall in payment is added to the unpaid principal balance of the loan.

Neglect—The failure to provide the proper care needed to avoid harm or illness.

Negligence—The failure to exercise the degree of care that a reasonable person would exercise given the same circumstances.

Negligence Per Se—Conduct, whether of action or omission, which may be declared and treated as negligence without any argument or proof as to the particular surrounding circumstances, because it is contrary to the law.

Negotiable Instrument—A signed writing that contains an unconditional promise to pay a sum of money, either on demand or at a specified time, payable to the order of the bearer.

Negotiation—The process in which the parties to a dispute communicate their differences to each other in an attempt to resolve them without court intervention.

Net Assets—Total assets minus total liabilities.

Net Estate—The gross estate less the decedent's debts, funeral expenses, and any other deductions authorized by law.

Net Income—Gross income less deductions and exemptions authorized by law.

Net Loss—The excess of all expenses and losses for a period over all revenues and gains of the same period.

Net Worth—The difference between one's assets and liabilities.

No-Asset Case—A chapter 7 bankruptcy case where there are no assets available to satisfy any portion of the creditors unsecured claims.

No-Fault Laws—The insurance laws that provide compensation to any person injured as a result of an automobile accident, regardless of fault.

No-Fault Divorce—A divorce that is granted without the necessity of finding a spouse to have been guilty of some marital misconduct.

Nolo Contendere—Latin for "I do not wish to contend." Statement by a defendant who does not wish to contest a charge. Although tantamount to a plea of guilty for the offense charged, it cannot be used against the defendant in another forum.

Nominal Damages—A trivial sum of money which is awarded as recognition that a legal injury was sustained, although slight.

Non-Assumption Clause—A statement in a mortgage contract forbidding the assumption of the mortgage by another borrower without the prior approval of the lender.

Non Obstante Verdicto (N.O.V.)—Latin for "notwithstanding the verdict." Refers to a judgment of the court that reverses the jury's verdict, based on the judge's determination that the verdict has no basis in law, or is unsupported by the facts.

Non Sequitur—Latin for "it does not follow." Refers to something that is illogically placed in the sequence or progression of events.

Nonconforming Use—The use of land which no longer complies with zoning regulations, although it was a lawful use prior to the implementation of such regulations.

Nondischargeable Debt—A debt that cannot be eliminated in bankruptcy.

Nonfeasance—In the law of agency, refers to the absolute failure of the agent to perform a duty for the principal that the agent previously promised to do.

Nonfreehold Estate—A leasehold.

Nonimmigrant—An alien who enters the United States with the intention of leaving following completion of a stay for a limited time period and purpose.

North American Free-Trade Agreement (NAFTA)—Public Law 103-182 (Act of 12/8/93), superseded the United States-Canada Free-Trade Agreement effective 1/1/94. It continues the special, reciprocal trading relationship between the United States and Canada, and establishes a similar relationship with Mexico.

Not Guilty—The plea of a defendant in a criminal action denying the offense with which he or she is charged.

Notary Public—A public officer authorized to administer oaths, certify certain documents, and take depositions.

Note—Legal document obligating a borrower to repay a loan at a stated interest rate during a specified period of time.

Note of Issue—A document filed with the court placing a cause on the trial calendar.

Notice of Default—Written notice to a borrower that a default has occurred and that legal action may be taken.

Notice of Entry—A notice with an affidavit of service stating that the attached copy of an entered order or judgment has been served by a party on another party.

Notice of Petition—Written notice of a petitioner that a hearing will be held in a court to determine the relief requested in an annexed petition.

Novation—A novation refers to the substitution of a new party and the discharge of an original party to a contract, with the assent of all parties.

Nuisance—The disturbance of another's use of their property, rendering continued use uncomfortable or inconvenient.

Nunc Pro Tunc—Latin for "now for then." Refers to the retroactive effect given some action that should have been taken at an earlier point in time.

Nursing Home—A residential facility that gives nursing care or custodial care to an ill or injured person.

Nursing Home Abuse—The infliction of physical pain or injury on a nursing home resident by a person having care or custody over the resident.

Nursing Home Negligence—The failure to exercise the requisite standard of care in connection with the treatment and supervision of a nursing home resident.

Nursing Home Reform Act of 1987—Federal law governing nursing homes that gives nursing home residents certain rights.

O

Oath—A sworn declaration of the truth under penalty of perjury.

Objection—The process by which it is asserted that a particular question, or piece of evidence, is improper, and it is requested that the court rule upon the objectionable matter.

Objection to Discharge—In a bankruptcy proceeding, a trustee's or creditor's objection to the debtor being released from personal liability for certain dischargeable debts.

Objection to Exemption—In a bankruptcy proceeding, a trustee's or creditor's objection to the debtor's attempt to claim certain property as exempt from liquidation by the trustee to creditors.

Obligee—One who is entitled to receive a sum of money or performance from the obligor.

Obligor—One who promises to perform or pay a sum of money under a contract.

Obscene Material—Material which lacks serious literary, artistic, political, or scientific value and, taken as a whole, appeals to the prurient interest and, as such, is not protected by the free speech guarantee of the First Amendment.

Obstruction of Justice—An offense by which one hinders the process by which individuals seek justice in the court, such as by intimidating jury members.

Occupational Disease—A disease or infection arising out of and occurring in the course and scope of employment, that is caused by substances or activities to which an employee is not ordinarily subjected or exposed other than during employment, and requires medical services or results in disability or death.

Occupational Safety and Health Act (OSHA)—A law passed by Congress in 1970 to protect employees from injury or illness in the course of their employment by enforcing safety and health standards.

Occupational Safety and Health Administration (OSHA)—The federal agency that oversees workplace safety and health in federal offices and in states without state OSHA programs.

Of Counsel—An attorney who is not the principal attorney of record, but who aids the principal attorney in preparation of a case.

Offense—Any misdemeanor or felony violation of the law for which a penalty is prescribed.

Offer—A manifestation of willingness to enter into a bargain that invites the acceptance of the person to whom the offer is made.

Offeree—The person to whom an offer is made.

Offeror—The person who makes an offer.

Ombudsman—Under certain state laws, an individual licensed to oversee various health care issues.

Opening Statement—The first address of counsel prior to offering of evidence.

Opinion—The reasoning behind a court's decision.

Opt-In—Refers to when a user gives explicit permission for a company to use personal information for marketing purposes.

Opt-Out—Refers to when a user prohibits a company from using personal information for marketing purposes.

Option—A right to purchase or lease property at an agreed upon price and terms within a specified time, which is given in return for some consideration, usually monetary.

Option Contract—In real estate law, a binding agreement whereby the owner agrees to sell the property to a prospective purchaser, at a specified price, within a stated period of time.

Oral Agreement—An oral agreement is one that is not in writing or not signed by the parties.

Oral Proof—Evidence given by word of mouth; the oral testimony of a witness.

Order—An oral or written direction of a court or judge.

Order of Protection—An order issued by a court that directs one individual to stop certain conduct, such as harassment, against another individual and that may order the individual to be excluded from the residence and to stay away from the other individual, his or her home, school, place of employment, and his or her children.

Ordinance—A local law passed by a municipal legislative body.

Original Jurisdiction—The jurisdiction of a court to hear a matter in the first instance.

Origination Fee—Fee charged by a mortgage lender to cover administrative costs of processing a mortgage loan.

Orphan—A minor child whose parents have died, have relinquished their parental rights, or whose parental rights have been terminated by a court of jurisdiction.

Outlying Areas—Includes the United States Virgin Islands, Guam, American Samoa, and the Commonwealth of the Northern Mariana Islands.

Overrule—A holding in a particular case is overruled when the same court, or a higher court, in that jurisdiction, makes an opposite ruling in a subsequent case on the identical point of law ruled upon in the prior case.

Oyez—The term meaning "hear ye" which is used by the bailiff at the beginning of the court proceeding.

P

Pain and Suffering—Refers to damages recoverable against a wrong-doer that include physical or mental suffering.

Palimony—An award of support that arises out of the dissolution of a nonmarital relationship.

Paralegal—An individual usually employed by a law office to perform various tasks associated with the practice of law, but one who is not licensed to practice law.

Paramount Title—Refers to title that is superior over any other claim of title.

Parcel—A tract or a plot of land.

Pardon—To release from further punishment, either conditionally or unconditionally.

Parens Patriae—Latin for "parent of his country." Refers to the role of the state as guardian of legally disabled individuals.

Parol Evidence Rule—The doctrine that holds that the written terms of an agreement may not be varied by prior or oral agreements.

Parole—The conditional release from imprisonment whereby the convicted individual serves the remainder of his or her sentence outside of prison, as long as he or she is in compliance with the terms and conditions of parole.

Part—A courtroom where specified business of a court is to be conducted by a judicial officer.

Partition—A division of real property among co-owners.

Partnership—An agreement between two or more persons to conduct a business for profit.

Party—Person having a direct interest in a legal matter, transaction, or proceeding. The disputant.

Party in Interest—A party who has standing to be heard by the court in a matter to be decided in a bankruptcy case.

Passport—An official document which proves the identity and nationality of the person for whom it was issued.

Patent—A patent secures the exclusive right to make, use and sell an invention for 17 years.

Paternity—The relationship of fatherhood.

Paternity Testing—Genetic testing that can determine the identity of the biological father.

Payment Cap—Consumer safeguards that limit the amount monthly payments on an adjustable-rate mortgage may change. Since they do not limit the amount of interest the lender is earning, they may cause negative amortization.

Pecuniary—A term relating to monetary matters.

Peers—Those who are a man's equals in rank and station.

Penal Institution—A place of confinement for convicted criminals.

Pendente Lite—Latin for "while the action is pending." Refers to legal matters that are pending until, and contingent upon, the outcome of the lawsuit.

Pension Plan—A retirement plan established by an employer for the payment of pension benefits to employees upon retirement.

Per Diem Interest—Interest calculated per day.

Peremptory Challenge—The challenge that may be used to reject a certain number of prospective jurors without assigning any reason.

Perfected Appeal—Refers to the satisfaction of all of the necessary steps for an appellant to proceed with his or her appeal in the appellate court.

Performance—Performance refers to the completion of one's contractual obligation.

Periodic Rental Agreement—An oral or written rental agreement that states the length of time between rent payments, e.g., a week or a month, but not the total number of weeks or months that the agreement will be in effect.

Perjury—A crime where a person under oath swears falsely in a matter material to the issue or point in question.

Permanent Residence—In immigration law, refers to the status of having been lawfully accorded the privilege of residing permanently in the United States as an immigrant in accordance with the immigration laws, such status not having changed.

Permanent Resident Alien—An alien admitted to the United States as a lawful permanent resident.

Person—An individual, corporation, business trust, estate, trust, partnership, association, joint venture, government, governmental subdivision or agency, or any other legal or commercial entity.

Personal Information—As it relates to identity theft, refers to information associated with an actual person or a fictitious person that is a name, an address, a telephone number, an electronic mail address, a driver's license number, a social security number, an employer, a place of employment, information related to employment, an employee identification number, a mother's maiden name, an identifying number of a depository account, a bank account number, a password used for accessing information, or any other name, number, or code that is used, alone or in conjunction with other information, to confirm the identity of an actual or a fictitious person.

Personal Jurisdiction—The power of a court over the person of a defendant.

Personal Property—All property that is not real property.

Personal Service—Handing a copy of court papers directly to the person to be served.

Personal Surety Bond—Bond executed by a guardian, and sureties willing to vouch for the guardian, that allows the court to seek restitution from the guardian or sureties, if the guardian does not perform his or her duties.

Personally Identifiable Information—See **PII**.

Petit Jury—The ordinary jury for the trial of a civil case as distinguished from a grand jury.

Petition—A formal written request to a court that initiates a special proceeding.

Petitioner—One who presents a petition to a court or other body either in order to institute an equity proceeding or to take an appeal from a judgment.

Piercing the Corporate Veil—The process of holding another liable, such as an individual, for the acts of a corporation.

PII—Acronym for Personally Identifiable Information—refers to information such as name, mailing address, phone number or email address.

Piracy—The illegal reproduction and distribution of property that is protected by copyright, patent, trademark, or trade secret law.

PITI—Acronym for Principal, Interest, Taxes, and Insurance, the components of a monthly mortgage payment.

Plagiarism—The appropriation of another's literary works by claiming credit for having produced those works on one's own.

Plain View—In criminal law, refers to the exception to the search and seizure laws whereby an object in plain sight of the police may be seized without a search warrant.

Plaintiff—In a civil proceeding, the one who initially brings the lawsuit.

Plat—A map that shows the location of real estate within a town or county.

Plea Bargaining—The process of negotiating a disposition of a case to avoid a trial of the matter.

Pleadings—Refers to plaintiff's complaint that sets forth the facts of the cause of action, and defendant's answer that sets forth the responses and defenses to the allegations contained in the complaint.

Points—Fees paid to a mortgage lender for the loan. One point equals 1 percent of the mortgage loan amount.

Police Power—The power of the state to restrict private individuals in matters relating to public health, safety, and morality, and to impose such other restrictions as may be necessary to promote the welfare of the general public.

Polling the Jury—A practice whereby the jurors are asked individually whether they assented, and still assent, to the verdict.

Polygraph—A lie detector test.

Poor Person Application—An application made to the court, by either the plaintiff or defendant, stating that because of insufficient income, he or she is unable to pay the court fees normally required for certain legal actions. If the application is granted by the court, the usual court costs for the action are waived.

Port of Entry—Any location in the United States or its territories that is designated as a point of entry for aliens and U.S. Citizens.

Portfolio—The entirety of one's financial investments.

Pose—As it relates to identity theft, means to falsely represent oneself, directly or indirectly, as another person or persons.

Post Mortem—Latin for "after death." Refers to the coroner's examination of a body to determine cause of death.

Post-Petition Transfer—In a bankruptcy proceeding, a transfer of the debtor's property made after the commencement of the case.

Poverty Guidelines—The list published annually by the Department of Health and Human Services that gives the lowest income acceptable for a family of a particular size so that the family does not live in poverty.

Power of Attorney—A legal document authorizing another to act on one's behalf.

Pre-Approval—The process of determining how much money a prospective homebuyer or refinancer will be eligible to borrow prior to application for a loan, including a preliminary review of a borrower's credit report.

Pre-Bankruptcy Planning—The arrangement of a debtor's property to allow the debtor to take maximum advantage of exemptions.

Pre-Inspection—Complete immigration inspection of airport passengers before departure from a foreign country.

Pre-Petition—Occurrences which take place before a petition is filed in bankruptcy court.

Pre-Qualification—The process of determining how much money a prospective homebuyer will be eligible to borrow prior to application for a mortgage loan.

Precedent—A previously decided case that is recognized as authority for the disposition of future cases.

Preclude—To prevent or stop.

Preexisting Condition—A condition that existed before the compensable injury or disease.

Preferential Debt Payment—A debt payment made to a creditor in the 90-day period before a debtor files bankruptcy that gives the creditor more than the creditor would receive in the debtor's chapter 7 case.

Premeditation—The deliberate contemplation of an act prior to committing it.

Premium—The periodic payment of money by an insured to an insurer for insurance protection against specified losses.

Prenuptial Agreement—An agreement entered into by prospective spouses prior to and in contemplation of marriage.

Prepaid Expenses—Taxes, insurance and assessments paid in advance of their due dates.

Prepaid Interest—Interest that is paid in advance of when it is due which is typically charged to a borrower at closing to cover interest on the loan between the closing date and the first payment date.

Prepayment—Full or partial repayment of loan principal before the contractual due date.

Prepayment Penalty—A penalty payable by a borrower for early payment of a debt.

Presumption of Innocence—In criminal law, refers to the doctrine that an individual is considered innocent of a crime until he or she is proven guilty.

Prima Facie Case—A case which is sufficient on its face, being supported by at least the requisite minimum of evidence, and being free from palpable defects.

Prime Rate—Preferential rate of interest on loans given to large and regular borrowers by banks.

Principal—The amount of debt, not counting interest, left on a loan.

Principal Alien—An alien who has qualified for U.S. Permanent Residence directly, and not derivatively.

Prisoner—One who is confined to a prison or other penal institution for the purpose of awaiting trial for a crime, or serving a sentence after conviction of a crime.

Privacy Policy—A privacy policy is a statement describing what information about the user is collected and how it is used; also known as a privacy statement or privacy notice.

Private Mortgage Insurance (PMI)—Insurance to protect the lender in case you default on your loan, generally not required with conventional loans if the down payment is at least 20%.

Privity of Contract—The relationship between the parties to a contract.

Pro Hac Vice—Latin for "for this turn." Refers to the permission granted an out-of-state lawyer to appear in another state's courts.

Pro-Rata Basis—Proportionately.

Pro Se—Latin for "for oneself." Refers to a party who acts as his or her own attorney without formal legal representation.

Probable Cause—The standard which must be met in order for there to be a valid search and seizure or arrest. It includes the showing of facts and circumstances reasonably sufficient and credible to permit the police to obtain a warrant.

Probate—The process of proving the validity of a will and administering the estate of a decedent.

Probate Court—Court with statutory authority to hear probate matters.

Probative Evidence—Evidence that has a tendency to prove or to actually prove an issue.

Process—A legal means, such as a summons, used to subject a defendant in a lawsuit to the jurisdiction of the court.

Process Server—A person who serves court papers on a party to a suit.

Procreation—The generation of children.

Product Liability—The legal liability of manufacturers and sellers to compensate buyers, users, and even bystanders, for damages or injuries suffered because of defects in goods purchased.

Professional Associations—Non-profit, cooperative and voluntary organizations that are designed to help their members in dealing with problems of mutual interest.

Professional Guardian—A public or private agency or organization that provides guardianship and/or conservatorship services, and receives compensation.

Professional Malpractice—The failure of one rendering professional services to exercise that degree of skill and learning commonly applied in the community by the average prudent reputable member of the profession, with the result of injury, loss or damage to the recipient of those services, or to those entitled to rely upon them.

Promissory Note—A written promise by the maker to pay a certain sum of money to the payee or his order on demand or on a fixed date.

Proof of Service—A form that must be completed by the person serving court papers on a party, stating that service was properly made.

Property Line—The official dividing line between properties.

Property of the Estate—In a bankruptcy proceeding, all legal or equitable interests of the debtor in property as of the commencement of the case.

Proprietorship—The most common legal form of business ownership comprising about 85 percent of all small businesses and whereby the liability of the owner is unlimited.

Prosecution—The process of pursuing a civil lawsuit or a criminal trial.

Prosecutor—The individual who prepares a criminal case against an individual accused of a crime.

Prospectus—A document given by a company to prospective investors, which sets forth all the material information concerning the company and its financial stability, so the investor can make an informed decision on whether to invest in it.

Protected Person—A minor or individual for whom a conservator has been appointed or for whom other protective orders have been issued.

Provocation—The act of inciting another to do a particular deed.

Proximate Cause—That which, in a natural and continuous sequence, unbroken by any efficient intervening cause, produces injury, and without which the result would not have occurred.

Prurient Interest—The shameful and morbid interest in nudity and sex.

Public Defender—A lawyer hired by the government to represent an indigent person accused of a crime.

Punitive Damages—Compensation in excess of compensatory damages that serves as a form of punishment to the wrongdoer who has exhibited malicious and willful misconduct.

Purchase Agreement—Contract signed by buyer and seller stating the terms and conditions under which a property will be sold.

Purchase Order—A document that authorizes a seller to deliver goods, and is considered an offer that is accepted upon delivery.

Purge—To atone for an offense or submit to a court's mandate.

Putative Father—Legal term for the alleged or supposed father of a child.

Putative Father Registries—Registry system that serves to ensure that a birth father's rights are protected.

Q

Quantum Meruit—Latin for "as much as is deserved." An equitable doctrine based on unjust enrichment which refers to the extent of liability in a contract implied by law, wherein the court infers a reasonable amount payable by the willing recipient of services rendered or goods furnished.

Quash—To annul or vacate, for example, a subpoena.

Quasi-Contract—Quasi contract refers to the legal obligation invoked in the absence of an agreement where there has been unjust enrichment.

Question of Fact—The fact in dispute that is the province of the trier of fact, i.e., the judge or jury, to decide.

Question of Law—The question of law that is the province of the judge to decide.

Quid Pro Quo—Latin for "something for something." Refers to the exchange of promises or performances between two parties. Also refers to the legal consideration necessary to create a binding contract.

Quiet Enjoyment—The right of an owner or lessor to have unimpaired use and enjoyment out of the property.

Quiet Title—Refers to an action to determine proper title to a specific piece of property.

Quitclaim Deed—A deed that conveys only that right, title or interest, if any, which the grantor may have in a piece of property.

Quorum—The number of members, usually a majority, whose presence is necessary in order for business to be transacted.

R

Racketeering—An organized conspiracy to commit extortion.

Rape—The unlawful sexual intercourse with a female person without her consent.

Ratification—In agency law, refers to the voluntary decision to confirm the acts of another thus accepting the responsibility for the consequences of those acts.

Rational Basis Test—The constitutional analysis of a law to determine whether it has a reasonable relationship to some legitimate government objective so as to uphold the law.

Reaffirmation Agreement—In a bankruptcy proceeding, an agreement by a chapter 7 debtor to continue paying a dischargeable debt after the bankruptcy, usually for the purpose of keeping the collateral that would otherwise be subject to repossession.

Real Estate—The land and all the things permanently attached to it.

Real Property—Land, and, generally, whatever is erected or growing upon, or affixed to the land.

Reargument—The presentation of additional oral argument to the court prior to its decision on an issue, but after the original argument has been heard, in order to present a new or overlooked principle of law or fact.

Reasonable Doubt—The standard of certainty of guilt a juror must have in order to find a defendant guilty of the crime charged.

Rebuttal—The opportunity of each party to refute the other party's claims.

Reciprocity—A relationship between individuals, states or countries whereby privileges granted by one side are returned by the other side.

Reconsideration—The procedure of requesting a governmental agency to reexamine their previous decision in the same case.

Reconstituted Family—A family in which the original parent has divorced and remarried.

Reconveyance—The transfer of property back to the owner when a mortgage loan is fully repaid.

Recording—The process of filing of certain legal instruments or documents with the appropriate government office.

Recrimination—A counter-charge of adultery or cruelty made by the accused spouse in a suit for divorce against the accusing spouse.

Recuse—To disqualify oneself as a judge.

Red Herring—The term used to describe an issue raised in a lawsuit which may have general importance but which has no relevance to the issue being determined.

Redact—To edit or revise.

Redlining—An illegal form of discrimination whereby a lender denies credit based on the characteristics of the borrower's neighborhood.

Referee—An individual who is appointed by the court for a specific issue and empowered to determine issues of fact for the purpose of reporting to the court concerning the particular issue, so that the court can render a judgment.

Referee's Deed—A deed given by a referee or other public officer pursuant to a court order for the sale of property.

Refinancing—The process of paying off one mortgage loan with the proceeds from a new mortgage loan secured by the same property.

Reformation—An equitable remedy that calls for the rewriting of a contract involving a mutual mistake or fraud.

Refugee—Any person who is outside his or her country of nationality who is unable or unwilling to return to that country because of persecution or a well-founded fear of persecution.

Refugee Approvals—The number of refugees approved for admission to the United States during a fiscal year.

Refugee Arrivals—The number of refugees initially admitted to the United States through ports of entry during a fiscal year.

Refugee Authorized Admissions—The maximum number of refugees allowed to enter the United States in a given fiscal year.

Rehabilitation Act of 1973—A disability discrimination statute that preceded and served as a model for the Americans with Disabilities Act (ADA).

Reinstatement—Refers to the return of an employee to employment from which he or she was illegally dismissed.

Release—A document signed by one party, releasing claims he or she may have against another party, usually as part of a settlement agreement.

Relief—The remedies afforded a complainant by the court.

Relief from Forfeiture—An order by a court in an unlawful detainer—i.e., eviction—lawsuit that allows the losing tenant to remain in the rental unit, based on the tenant's ability to pay all of the rent that is due, or to otherwise fully comply with the lease.

Remand—To send a case back from an appellate court to the lower court from which it came, for further proceedings.

Remedy—Refers to the means by which a right is enforced or a violation of a right is compensated.

Remittitur—Legal process by which an appellate court transmits to the court below the proceedings before it, together with its decision, for such further action and entry of judgment as is required by the decision of the appellate court.

Removal of Barriers to Remarriage—Refers to the removal of religious barriers to remarriage when the marriage was solemnized in a religious ceremony by a clergyman or minister of any religion.

Rent Control Ordinances—Laws in some communities that limit or prohibit rent increases, or that limit the circumstances in which a tenant can be evicted.

Rent Withholding—The tenant's remedy of not paying some or all of the rent if the landlord does not fix defects that make the rental unit uninhabitable within a reasonable time after the landlord receives notice of the defects from the tenant.

Rental Agreement—An oral or written agreement between a tenant and a landlord, made before the tenant moves in, which establishes the terms of the tenancy, such as the amount of the rent and when it is due.

Rental Application—A form that a landlord may ask a tenant to fill out prior to renting that requests information about the tenant, such as the tenant's address, telephone number, employment history, credit references, etc.

Rental Period—The length of time between rental payments; for example, a week or a month.

Rental Unit—An apartment, house, duplex, or condominium that a landlord rents to a tenant to live in.

Renter's Insurance—Insurance protecting the tenant against property losses, such as losses from theft or fire. This insurance usually also protects the tenant against liability for claims or lawsuits filed by the landlord or by others alleging that the tenant negligently injured another person or property.

Reopening—The procedure of adding additional facts or documentation to the record of a case after it has been closed.

Repair and Deduct Remedy—The tenant's remedy of deducting from future rent the amount necessary to repair defects covered by the implied warranty of habitability. The amount deducted cannot be more than one month's rent.

Replevin—An action brought for the owner of items to recover possession of those items when those items were wrongfully taken, or are being wrongfully kept.

Reply—A plaintiff's response to a defendant's answer when the answer contains a counterclaim.

Repudiation—In contract law, refers to the declaration of one of the parties to the contract that he or she will not perform under the contract.

Res—Latin for "the thing." Refers to the subject matter of a legal action.

Res Ipsa Loquitur—Latin for "the thing speaks for itself." Refers to an evidentiary rule which provides that negligence may be inferred from the fact that an accident occurred when such an occurrence would not ordinarily have happened in the absence of negligence, the cause of the occurrence was within the exclusive control of the defendant, and the plaintiff was in no way at fault.

Res Judicata—Latin for "the thing has been decided." Refers to the doctrine whereby a final judgment rendered in an action is binding on the parties to any subsequent litigation involving the same claim.

Rescission—The cancellation of a contract that returns the parties to the positions they were in before the contract was made.

Resettlement—Permanent relocation of refugees in a place outside their country of origin to allow them to establish residence and become productive members of society there.

Residence—In immigration law, refers to an alien's actual dwelling place in fact, without regard to intent.

Residuary Clause—The clause in a will that conveys to the residuary beneficiaries any property of the testator that was not specifically given to a particular legatee.

RESPA—The Real Estate Settlement Procedures Act, a federal law that gives consumers the right to review information about loan settlement costs.

Respondent—The responding party, also known as the defendant.

Response—Also referred to as an Answer, Defendant's statement as to why a claim is not true or is inaccurate as to amount.

Restatement of Contracts—The Restatement of Contracts is a series of volumes written and published by the American Law Institute (ALI) which attempts to state an orderly explanation of the current and evolving law of contracts.

Restatement of the Law—A series of volumes authored by the American Law Institute that tell what the law in a general area is, how it is changing, and what direction the authors think this change should take.

Restitution—The act of making an aggrieved party whole by compensating him or her for any loss or damage sustained.

Restore to Calendar—To reinstate the action to active status.

Retainer Agreement—A contract between an attorney and the client stating the nature of the services to be rendered and the cost of the services.

Returning Residents—Lawful permanent residents who want to return to the United States after staying abroad more than one year or beyond the expiration of their re-entry permits.

Revocation of a Visa—Cancellation of a visa rendering it invalid for travel to the United States.

Right of Election—In probate law, refers to the right of a surviving spouse to take his or her share of the estate of the deceased, either under the terms of the will or as provided by statute.

Right of Rescission—Under the provisions of the Truth-in-Lending Act, the borrower's right, on certain kinds of loans, to cancel the loan within three days of signing a mortgage.

Right of Survivorship—The automatic succession to the interest of a deceased joint owner in a joint tenancy.

Riparian Rights—The rights afforded owners of land located adjacent to waterways, e.g., to use the water.

Robbery—The felonious act of stealing from a person, by the use of force or the threat of force, so as to put the victim in fear.

S

Safe Haven—Temporary refuge given to migrants who have fled their countries of origin to seek protection or relief from persecution or other hardships, until they can return to their countries safely or, if necessary, until they can obtain permanent relief from the conditions they fled.

Sale—An agreement to transfer property from the seller to the buyer for a stated sum of money.

Sale and Leaseback—An agreement whereby the seller transfers property to the buyer who immediately leases the property back to the seller.

Sales Agreement—Contract signed by buyer and seller stating the terms and conditions under which a property will be sold.

Sanction—A form of punishment.

Satisfaction—The discharge and release of an obligation.

Scope of Authority—In agency law, refers to the actions which have been actually, apparently or impliedly delegated to the agent.

Scope of Employment—Those activities performed while carrying out the business of one's employer.

Seal—An impression on a document which serves to formally attest to the execution of the document; also refers to the practice of closing a case file from public scrutiny in certain instances, e.g., cases involving minors, and acquittals.

Sealing Orders—Orders issued by the court to prevent the public from obtaining information on sealed cases.

Search and Seizure—The search by law enforcement officials of a person or place in order to seize evidence to be used in the investigation and prosecution of a crime.

Search Warrant—A judicial order authorizing and directing law enforcement officials to search a specified location for specific items or individuals.

Second Mortgage—An additional mortgage placed on a property that has rights that are subordinate to the first mortgage.

Secured Credit Card—A credit card secured by a savings deposit to ensure payment of the outstanding balance if the credit card holder defaults on payments.

Secured Creditor—An individual or business holding a claim against the debtor that is secured by a lien on property of the estate, or that is subject to a right of setoff.

Secured Debt—Debt backed by a mortgage, pledge of collateral, or other lien.

Secured Loan—Borrowed money backed by collateral.

Secured Party—A lender, seller, or other person in whose favor there is a security interest, including a person to whom accounts or chattel paper have been sold.

Security Deposit—A deposit or a fee that the landlord requires the tenant to pay at the beginning of the tenancy to protect the landlord, for example, if the tenant moves out owing rent, or leaves the rental unit damaged or less clean than when the tenant moved in.

Sedition—An illegal act that tends to cause disruption of the government.

Segregation—The separation of persons or things from other persons or things.

Seised—The status of lawfully owning and possessing real property.

Selective Emancipation—The doctrine under which a child is deemed emancipated for only a part of the period of minority, or from only a part of the parent's rights, or for some purposes, and not for others.

Selective Service—Governmental department requiring registration of male aliens aged 18 to 26.

Self-Defense—The right to protect oneself, one's family, and one's property from an aggressor.

Sentence—The punishment given a convicted criminal by the court.

Separate Property—Property owned by a married person in his or her own right during marriage.

Separation Agreement—Written arrangements concerning custody, child support, spousal support, and property division usually made by a married couple who decide to live separate and apart in contemplation of divorce.

Separation of Powers—The doctrine that prohibits one branch of the government from exercising the powers belonging to another branch of government.

Sequester—Generally, to separate from, such as a jury during trial.

Service by Publication—When service of process is done by publishing a notice in a newspaper after a court determines that other means of service are impractical or have been unsuccessful.

Service of Process—The delivery of legal court documents, such as a complaint, to the defendant.

Session Laws—Laws enacted by a state legislature that are generally bound in volumes according to the order of their enactment.

Settlement—An agreement by the parties to a dispute on a resolution of the claims, usually requiring some mutual action, such as payment of money, in consideration of a release of claims.

Settlement Costs—Also known as closing costs, refers to the costs for services that must be performed before the loan can be initiated, such as title fees, recording fees, appraisal fee, credit report fee, pest inspection, attorney's fees, and surveying fees.

Severalty—Ownership by a person in his or her own right.

Severance Pay—Monies paid to a terminated employee.

Sexual Abuse—Nonconsensual sexual contact.

Sexual Harassment—Any unwelcome sexual advance, request for sexual favors, or verbal, written or physical conduct of a sexual nature by a manager, supervisor, or co-worker.

Shareholder—A person who owns shares of stock in a corporation.

Sherman Antitrust Act—A federal statute passed in 1890 to prohibit monopolization and unreasonable restraint of trade in interstate and foreign commerce.

Short Form Order—An order prepared by the court.

Show Cause Order—An accelerated method of starting an action, brought on by motion, which compels the opponent to respond within a shorter time period than usual.

Sibling—Brother or sister.

Silent Partner—An investor in a business who is either unidentified to third parties, or who does not take an active role in day-to-day management of the business.

Sine Die—Latin for "without day." Refers to an action that is adjourned indefinitely, without a set future date to convene.

Single Parent Family—A family in which one parent remains the primary caretaker of the children, and the children maintain little or no contact with the other parent.

Slander—Spoken words that are damaging to the reputation of another.

Small Business Administration (SBA)—Organization whose fundamental purpose is to aid, counsel, assist, and protect the interest of small businesses.

Small Business Corporation—A corporation which satisfies the definition of I.R.C. §1371(a), §1244(c)(2) or both. Satisfaction of I.R.C. §1371(a) permits a Subchapter S election, while satisfaction of I.R.C. §1244 enables the shareholders of the corporation to claim an ordinary loss on the worthlessness of the stock.

Small Business Investment Act—Federal legislation enacted in 1958 under which investment companies may be organized for supplying long term equity capital to small businesses.

Small Claims Court—The division of the trial court that handles civil cases asking for damages below a prescribed limit, e.g., $5,000, which is intended to be more expedient and less costly than a regular civil lawsuit.

Social Security Administration—The federal agency that issues retirement and disability benefits to qualified individuals.

Sole Proprietorship—A business owned and managed by a single individual.

Sovereign Immunity—A doctrine that prohibits lawsuits against the government without its consent.

Special Proceedings—General term for remedies or proceedings that are not ordinary actions, e.g., condemnation.

Special Term—A court part set aside to hear specific types of cases.

Special Verdict—A special finding of the facts of a case by a jury leaving to the court the application of the law to the facts thus found.

Specific Performance—The equitable remedy requiring the party who breaches a contract to perform his or her obligations under the contract.

Spending Power—The power given Congress to spend money to provide for the general welfare of the United States.

Sponsored Immigrant—An immigrant who has had an affidavit of support filed for him or her.

Spousal Maintenance—Money paid by one spouse to another for living expenses.

Spouse—Legally married husband or wife.

Standing—The legal right of an individual or group to use the courts to resolve an existing controversy.

State—Refers to each of the 50 States, the District of Columbia, the Commonwealth of Puerto Rico, and each of the outlying areas.

Statement of Financial Affairs—In a bankruptcy proceeding, a series of questions the debtor must answer in writing concerning such items as sources of income, transfers of property, and lawsuits by creditors.

Statement of Intention—In a bankruptcy proceeding, a declaration made by a chapter 7 debtor concerning plans for dealing with consumer debts that are secured by property of the estate.

Status Offender—A child who commits an act which is not criminal in nature, but which, nevertheless, requires some sort of intervention and disciplinary attention merely because of the age of the offender.

Statute—A law.

Statute of Frauds—Legal doctrine providing that all agreements concerning title to real estate must be in writing to be enforceable.

Statute of Limitations—Any law that fixes the time within which parties must take judicial action to enforce rights or thereafter be barred from enforcing them.

Statutory—Fixed by statute.

Stay—A judicial order suspending some action until further court order lifting the stay.

Stepchild—A spouse's child from a previous marriage or other relationship.

Stepparent Adoption—The adoption of a child by the new spouse of the birth parent.

Stipulation—An agreement by attorneys on opposite sides of a case as to any matter pertaining to the proceedings or trial.

Stipulation of Settlement—A formal agreement between litigants and/or their attorneys resolving their dispute.

Stock Certificate—A certificate issued to a shareholder that evidences partial ownership of the shareholder in a company.

Stowaway—An alien coming to the United States surreptitiously on an airplane or vessel without legal status of admission.

Strict Liability—A concept applied by the courts in product liability cases, in which a seller is liable for any and all defective or hazardous products that unduly threaten a consumer's personal safety.

Sua Sponte—Latin for "of itself." Refers to an action taken by the court upon its own motion and without the intervention of either party.

Subdivision—The division or a piece of land into two or more smaller pieces.

Sublease—A separate rental agreement between the original tenant and a new tenant to whom the original tenant rents all or part of the rental unit. The new tenant is called a subtenant. The agreement between the original tenant and the landlord remains in force, and the original tenant continues to be responsible for paying the rent to the landlord and for other tenant's obligations.

Submission—The filing of a dispute to a dispute resolution process.

Subordination—The status of a claim or debt that is behind, or lower in priority, to another claim or debt.

Subornation of Perjury—The criminal offense of procuring another to make a false statement under oath.

Subpoena—A court issued document compelling the appearance of a witness before the court.

Subpoena Duces Tecum—Derived from the Latin "duces tecum," meaning "you shall bring with you." Refers to a court issued document requiring a witness to produce certain documents in his or her possession or control.

Substantial Abuse—The characterization of a bankruptcy case filed by an individual whose debts are primarily consumer debts where the court finds that the granting of relief would be an abuse of chapter 7 because, for example, the debtor can pay its debts.

Substantial Performance—The performance of nearly all of the essential terms of a contract so that the purpose of the contract has been accomplished giving rise to the right to compensation.

Substantive Consolidation—In a bankruptcy proceeding, putting the assets and liabilities of two or more related debtors into a single pool to pay creditors.

Successful Conciliation—Refers to a charge with reasonable cause determination that is closed after successful conciliation. Successful conciliation results in substantial relief to the charging party and all others adversely affected by the discrimination.

Succession—The process by which a decedent's property is distributed, either by will or by the laws of descent and distribution.

Successor—One who takes the place of another and continues in their position.

Successor Guardian or Conservator—A person appointed by the court to succeed a guardian or conservator upon death, resignation, removal, or incapacity. A successor guardian or conservator may also act in the case of an emergency if the acting guardian or conservator is unavailable.

Suicide—The deliberate termination of one's existence.

Suit—A legal action or proceeding.

Sum Certain—Liquidated damages pursuant to contract, promissory note, law, etc.

Summary Judgment—A judgment of the court that disposes of a controversy, based upon a motion brought by one of the parties, which demonstrates that there are no existing factual disputes in issue that necessitate a jury determination.

Summation—The point in the trial when the attorney for each party sums up the evidence presented in the case, and makes their final argument as to their legal position.

Summons—A mandate requiring the appearance of the defendant in an action under penalty of having judgment entered against him for failure to do so.

Supplemental Security Income (SSI)—The government program awarding cash benefits to the needy, aged, blind, or otherwise qualifying disabled.

Supplementary Proceedings—Further inquiry, under court jurisdiction, after entry of judgment, to determine a means for enforcing the judgment against judgment debtor.

Suppression of Evidence—The refusal to produce or permit evidence for use in litigation, such as when there has been an illegal search and seizure of the evidence.

Supreme Court—In most jurisdictions, the Supreme Court is the highest appellate court, including the federal court system.

Surety—One who undertakes to pay money or perform in the event that the principal fails to do so.

Surrogate—A person appointed to act in place of another.

Survey—A measurement of land, prepared by a licensed surveyor, showing a property's boundaries, elevations, improvements, and relationship to surrounding tracts.

Survival Statute—A statute that preserves for a decedent's estate a cause of action for infliction of pain and suffering and related damages suffered up to the moment of death.

Surviving Parent—A child's living parent when the child's other parent is dead, and the living parent has not remarried.

Suspended Sentence—A sentence that is not executed contingent upon the defendant's observance of certain court-ordered terms and conditions.

Sweat Equity—Value added to a property in the form of labor or services of the owner rather than cash.

T

Taft-Hartley Act—Refers to the Labor-Management Relations Act of 1947, which was established to prescribe the legitimate rights of both employees and employers.

Taking the Fifth—The term given to an individual's right not to incriminate oneself under the Fifth Amendment.

Tangible Property—Property that is capable of being possessed, whether real or personal.

Tariff—A form of tax assessed against imported and exported goods.

Tax—A sum of money assessed upon one's income, property and purchases, for the purpose of supporting the government.

Tax Court—A federal administrative agency that acts as a court for the purposes of determining disputes between individuals and the Internal Revenue Service.

Tax Evasion—The intentional and fraudulent underpayment or non-payment of taxes legally due.

Tax-Exempt—A condition of the law in which an organization or people in certain kinds of work do not have to pay taxes which regular citizens or businesses must pay, such as religious organizations.

Tax Impound—Money paid to and held by a lender for annual tax payments.

Tax Lien—Claim against a property for unpaid taxes.

Tax Sale—Public sale of property by a government authority as a result of non-payment of taxes.

Taxable Estate—The decedent's gross estate less applicable statutory estate tax deductions, such as charitable deductions.

Tenancy—The tenant's exclusive right, created by a rental agreement between the landlord and the tenant, to use and possess the landlord's rental unit.

Tenancy at Will—The right to occupy property for an indefinite period of time.

Tenancy by the Entirety—A form of ownership available only to a husband and wife whereby they each are deemed to hold title to the whole property, with right of survivorship.

Tenancy in Common—An ownership of real estate by two or more persons, each of whom has an undivided fractional interest in the whole property, without any right of survivorship.

Tenant—A person who rents or leases a rental unit from a landlord. The tenant obtains the right to the exclusive use and possession of the rental unit during the lease or rental period.

Term—The period of time between the beginning loan date on the legal documents and the date the entire balance of the loan is due.

Terminal Illness—An incurable condition caused by injury, disease, or illness which, regardless of the application of life-sustaining procedures, would, within reasonable medical judgment, produce death, and where the application of life-sustaining procedures serve only to postpone the moment of death of the patient.

Terminally Ill Patient—A patient whose death is imminent or whose condition, to a reasonable degree of medical certainty, is hopeless unless he or she is artificially supported through the use of life-sustaining procedures, and which condition is confirmed by a physician who is qualified and experienced in making such a diagnosis.

Termination of Employment—Refers to cessation of employment, e.g., by quitting or dismissal.

Termination of Parental Rights—The legal process that involuntarily severs a parent's rights to a child.

Territory—A geographical area belonging to or under the jurisdiction of a governmental authority.

Terrorism—Under the Homeland Security Act of 2002, terrorism is defined as activity that involves an act dangerous to human life or potentially destructive of critical infrastructure or key resources and is a violation of the criminal laws of the United States or of any State or other subdivision of the United States in which it occurs and is intended to intimidate or coerce the civilian population or influence a government or affect the conduct of a government by mass destruction, assassination, or kidnapping.

Testamentary Appointment—An appointment of a guardian, conservator, or power of attorney made by a will.

Testamentary Guardian or Conservator—A person named in the will of one who has been appointed by the court as guardian or conservator to succeed the guardian or conservator upon death.

Testate—The state of dying with a valid will in place.

Testator—A male individual who makes and executes a will.

Testatrix—A female individual who makes and executes a will.

Testify—The offering of a statement in a judicial proceeding, under oath and subject to the penalty of perjury.

Testimony—The sworn statement made by a witness in a judicial proceeding.

Third-Party Action—A claim asserted by a defendant, designated a third-party plaintiff, against a person, known as a third-party defendant.

Thrift Institution—A general term for savings banks and savings and loan associations.

Time Is of the Essence—A clause in a contract that states that the specified time of performance is an essential term of the contract that, if breached, will serve to discharge the entire contract.

Title—Document that gives evidence of ownership of property. Also indicates the rights of ownership and possession of the property.

Title Company—A company that insures title to property.

Title Insurance—Refers to an insurance policy that protects the lender and/or buyer against loss due to disputes over ownership of a property.

Title Search—Examination of municipal records to ensure that the seller is the legal owner of a property, and that there are no liens or other claims against the property.

Title VII—Refers to Title VII of the Civil Rights Act of 1964 that prohibits discrimination in employment based on race, color, religion, sex or national origin.

Tort—A private or civil wrong or injury, other than breach of contract, for which the court will provide a remedy in the form of an action for damages.

Tort Claims Act—A statute passed by Congress that waives the government's sovereign immunity from tort liability.

Tortfeasor—A wrong-doer.

Tortious Conduct—Wrongful conduct, whether of act or omission, of such a character as to subject the actor to liability under the law of torts.

Trade Association—An organization established to benefit members of the same trade by informing them of issues and developments within the organization and about how changes outside the organization will affect them.

Trade Name—Any name used by a person to identify his or her business or vocation; commercial name.

Trademark—Refers to any mark, word, symbol or other device used by a manufacturer to identify its products.

Transcript—An official and certified copy of what transpired in court or at an out-of-court deposition.

Transfer—The removal of a cause from the jurisdiction of one court or judge to another by lawful authority.

Transfer Tax—Tax paid when title to property passes from one owner to another.

Transferred Intent—The doctrine which provides that if a defendant intends harm to A, but harms B instead, the intent is deemed transferred to B, as far as the defendant's liability to B in tort is concerned.

Transit Alien—An alien in immediate and continuous transit through the United States, with or without a visa, e.g., for the purpose of changing between airplane flights or between ships.

Treaty—In international law, refers to an agreement made between two or more independent nations.

Trespass—A tortious interference with another's property.

Trespasser—An individual who enters upon another's property without the owner's permission.

Trial—The judicial procedure whereby disputes are determined based on the presentation of issues of law and fact. Issues of fact are decided by the trier of fact, either the judge or jury, and issues of law are decided by the judge.

Trial Court—The court of original jurisdiction over a particular matter.

Trial Date—The date that the Plaintiff and Defendant must appear in Court.

Trial de Novo—A new trial.

Truancy—Willful and unjustified failure to attend school by one who is required to attend.

Trust—The transfer of property, real or personal, to the care of a trustee, with the intention that the trustee manages the property on behalf of another person.

Truth in Lending Act—A federal law that requires commercial lenders to provide applicants with detailed, accurate, and understandable information relating to the cost of credit, so as to permit the borrower to make an informed decision.

U

Ultrahazardous—In tort law, refers to an activity which involves such a risk of harm to individuals or their property, that it gives rise to strict liability for any damage caused as a result of the activity.

Unconscionable—Refers to a bargain so one-sided as to amount to an absence of meaningful choice on the part of one of the parties, together with terms that are unreasonably favorable to the other party.

Unconstitutional—Refers to a statute which conflicts with the United States Constitution rendering it void.

Uncontested Divorce—A divorce action in which the defendant does not respond to the summons, or otherwise agrees not to oppose the divorce.

Undersecured Claim—In a bankruptcy proceeding, a debt secured by property that is worth less than the full amount of the debt.

Undertaking—Deposit of a sum of money or filing of a bond in court.

Underwrite—In insurance law, it refers to the assumption of the risk of loss to the insured's person or property, by the insurer of the insurance policy.

Underwriting—In mortgage lending, the process of determining the risks involved in a particular loan and establishing suitable terms and conditions for the loan.

Undue Influence—The exertion of improper influence upon another for the purpose of destroying that person's free will in carrying out a particular act, such as entering into a contract.

Unfair Labor Practice—Any activities carried out by either a union or an employer that violate the National Labor Relations Act.

Unfit—Incompetent.

Uniform Commercial Code (UCC)—The UCC is a code of laws governing commercial transactions that was designed to bring uniformity to the laws of the various states.

Uniform Federal Accessibility Standard (UFAS)—Technical standard for accessible design of new construction and alterations pursuant to the Architectural Barriers Act.

Uniform Gifts to Minors Act (U.G.M.A)—The uniform law adopted by the states providing for a method of making a gift, in trust, to a minor.

Uniform Laws—Laws that have been approved by the Commissioners on Uniform State Laws, and which are proposed to all state legislatures for consideration and adoption.

Unilateral Contract—A contract whereby one party makes a promise to do or refrain from doing something in return for actual performance by the other party.

Uninhabitable—A rental unit which has such serious problems or defects that the tenant's health or safety is affected is "uninhabitable." A rental unit may be uninhabitable if it is not fit for human beings to live in, or if it fails to substantially comply with building and safety code standards that materially affect tenants' health and safety.

Union Shop—A workplace where all of the employees are members of a union.

United States-Canada Free-Trade Agreement—Public Law 100-449 (Act of 9/28/88) established a special, reciprocal trading relationship between the United States and Canada. The United States-Canada Free-Trade Agreement was superseded by the North American Free-Trade Agreement (NAFTA), effective 1/1/94.

United States Citizenship and Immigration Services (USCIS)—Agency under the jurisdiction of the Department of Homeland Security that is responsible for the approval of all immigrant and nonimmigrant petitions, the authorization of permission to work in the United States, the issuance of extensions of stay, and change or adjustment of an applicant's status while the applicant is in the United States.

United States Consul—An employee of the U.S. Department of State, located at a foreign consulate or embassy of the United States, whose duty it is to supervise the issuance of immigrant and nonimmigrant visas.

United States Department of Housing and Urban Development—The federal agency that enforces the federal fair housing law, which prohibits discrimination based on sex, race, religion, national or ethnic origin, familial status, or mental handicap.

United States Trustee—The representative of the U.S. Department of Justice who oversees bankruptcy cases and appoints trustees to administer the property of the bankruptcy estate.

Unlawful Detainer—In real estate law, the act of a tenant unlawfully retaining possession of the leased premises after the expiration of the lease.

Unlawful Detainer Action—A lawsuit brought by a landlord against a tenant to evict the tenant from rental property.

Unliquidated Claim—In a bankruptcy proceeding, a claim for which a specific value has not been determined.

Unreasonable Search and Seizure—A search and seizure that has not met the constitutional requirements under the Fourth and Fourteenth Amendment.

Unscheduled Debt—In a bankruptcy proceeding, a debt that should have been listed by the debtor in the schedules filed with the court but was not.

Unsecured Claim—In a bankruptcy proceeding, a claim or debt for which a creditor holds no special assurance of payment.

Unsecured Credit—Credit extended without collateral.

Unsecured Debt—Debt not guaranteed by the pledge of collateral, e.g., a credit card.

Unsecured Loan—An advance of money that is not secured by collateral.

Unsuccessful Conciliation—Refers to a charge with reasonable cause determination that is closed after efforts to conciliate the charge are unsuccessful. Pursuant to Commission policy, the field office will close the charge and review it for litigation consideration. Because "reasonable cause" has been found, an unsuccessful conciliation is considered a merit resolution.

Usurious Contract—A contract that imposes interest at a rate that exceeds the legally permissible rate.

Usury—An excessive rate of interest above the maximum permissible rate established by the state legislature.

V

VA Mortgage—Fixed-rate loan guaranteed by the U.S. Department of Veterans Affairs, designed to make housing affordable for eligible U.S. veterans. VA loans are available to veterans, reservists, active-duty personnel, and surviving spouses of veterans with 100% entitlement. Eligible veterans may be able to purchase a home with no down payment, no cash reserve, no application fee, and lower closing costs than other financing options.

Vacate—To render something void, such as a judgment.

Vagrancy—A minor offense that refers to individuals who loiter with no lawful purpose.

Variable Rate—Interest rate that changes periodically in relation to an index.

Variance—The authorization to improve or develop a particular property in a manner not authorized by the zoning ordinance.

Vendor—A seller.

Venire—Technically, a writ summoning persons to court to act as jurors.

Venue—Geographical place where some legal matter occurs or may be determined. Also refers to the geographical area within which a court has jurisdiction.

Verdict—The definitive answer given by the jury to the court concerning the matters of fact committed to the jury for their deliberation and determination.

Verification—The confirmation of the authenticity of a document, such as an affidavit.

Verification of Deposit (VOD)—Document signed by a borrower's bank or other financial institution verifying the borrower's account balance and history.

Verification of Employment (VOE)—Document signed by a borrower's employer verifying the borrower's position and salary.

Verified Answer—The defendant's response to the plaintiff's Verified Complaint.

Verified Complaint—The document containing the plaintiff's allegations against the defendant.

Vested—The right to receive, either at present or in the future, a certain benefit, such as a pension from an employer, without further conditions, such as continued employment.

Veteran—A person who served in the active military, naval, or air service and who was discharged or released from his or her service under conditions other than dishonorable.

Vexatious Litigation—A lawsuit brought with malice and without probable cause.

Vicarious Liability—In tort law, refers to the liability assessed against one party due to the actions of another party.

Vice Crimes—Illegal activities that offend the moral standards of the community, such as gambling and prostitution.

Visa—Allows a foreign citizen to travel to the United States port- entry and request permission of the U.S. immigration inspector to enter the United States.

Visa Applicant—A foreign citizen who is applying for a nonimmigrant or immigrant U.S. visa. The visa applicant may also be referred as a beneficiary for petition based visas.

Visa Appointment—The procedure by which an applicant for immigrant status appears before a U.S. Consul for determination of the alien's qualification for an immigrant visa.

Visa Waiver Program (VWP)—Program which allows citizens of certain selected countries, traveling temporarily to the United States under the nonimmigrant admission classes of visitors for pleasure and visitors for business, to enter the United States without obtaining nonimmigrant visas for a period of no more than 90 days.

Visitation—The right of one parent to visit children of the marriage under order of the court.

Vitiate—To make void.

Void—Having no legal force or binding effect.

Void for Vagueness—The term given a criminal statute that is so vague that persons of normal intelligence do not comprehend its application, thus rendering it void.

Voidable—That which may be declared void but is not absolutely void or void in itself.

Voir Dire—French "to speak the truth," or, literally, "to see, to speak." Refers to the questioning, prior to trial, of prospective jurors by the attorneys, and, on application of any party, by the judge, to see if any of them should be disqualified or removed by challenge or examination.

Voluntary Arbitration—Arbitration that occurs by mutual and free consent of the parties.

Voluntary Departure—The departure of an alien from the United States without an order of removal.

W

Waive—To sign a written document—a "waiver"—giving up a right, claim, privilege, etc. In order for a waiver to be effective, the person giving the waiver must do so knowingly, and must know the right, claim, privilege, etc., that he or she is giving up.

Waiver—Voluntary relinquishment or surrender of some right or privilege.

Walk-Through—A final inspection of a home to check for problems that may need to be corrected before closing.

Wanton—Extremely negligent or reckless.

Ward—A person over whom a guardian is appointed to manage his or her affairs.

Warrant—An official order directing that a certain act be undertaken, such as an arrest.

Warrantless Arrest—An arrest carried out without a warrant.

Warranty—An assurance by one party to a contract that a certain fact exists and may be relied upon by the other party to the contract.

Warranty Deed—A deed that guarantees that the grantor has title to the property to be conveyed, and which holds the grantor liable if there is later discovered a defect in the title.

Warranty of Fitness for a Particular Purpose—A warranty that goods purchased are suitable for the specific purpose of the buyer.

Warranty of Habitability—A warranty by a landlord that leased premises are without defects that would render the premises unusable.

Warranty of Merchantability—A warranty that goods purchased are fit for the general purpose for which they are being purchased.

Whistleblower—An employee who reports on violations of the law that occur in the workplace.

White Collar Crime—Refers to a class of non-violent offenses that have their basis in fraud and dishonesty.

Wildcat Strike—An unauthorized strike for which the union representing the workers disclaims responsibility.

Will—A legal document which a person executes setting forth their wishes as to the distribution of their property upon death.

With Prejudice—A dismissal of an action "with prejudice" bars any new suit brought on the same cause of action.

Without Prejudice—A dismissal of an action "without prejudice" allows a new suit to be brought on the same cause of action.

Witness—One who testifies to what he has seen, heard, or otherwise observed.

Work Product—The work done by an attorney on behalf of a client, in connection with pending litigation, which is generally not subject to discovery.

Work-Related Injury or Illness—An injury or illness that is causally related to one's employment.

Workers' Compensation—Refers to the benefits payable to claimants under a workers' compensation claim, such as lost wages, medical expenses, etc.

Workplace Harassment—Any unwelcome verbal, written or physical conduct that either denigrates or shows hostility or aversion towards a person on the basis of race, color, national origin, age, sex, religion, disability, marital status, or pregnancy that: (1) has the purpose or effect of creating an intimidating, hostile or offensive work environment; (2) has the purpose or effect of unreasonably interfering with an employee's work performance; or (3) affects an employee's employment opportunities or compensation.

Writ—An order issuing from a court of justice and requiring the performance of a specified act, or giving authority and commission to have it done.

Writ of Possession—A document issued by the court after the landlord wins an unlawful detainer lawsuit. The writ of possession is served on the tenant by the sheriff. The writ informs the tenant that the tenant must leave the rental unit within a certain number of days, or the sheriff will forcibly remove the tenant.

Wrongful Death Action—An action brought to recover damages for the death of a person caused by the wrongful act or neglect of another.

Wrongful Death Statute—A statute that creates a cause of action for any wrongful act, neglect, or default that causes death.

Wrongful Discharge—An unlawful dismissal of an employee.

Wrongful Life—In tort law, refers to the birth of a child that should not have occurred for some reason, e.g., the negligent performance of a sterilization procedure.

X

X—Refers to the mark that may be used to denote one's signature when the signer is unable to write his or her name.

Y

Yield—The current return on a stock or bond expressed in the form of a percentage.

Youthful Offender—An individual who is older than a juvenile but younger than an adult.

Z

Zone of Employment—The physical area within which injuries to an employee are covered by worker compensation laws.

Zoning—The government regulation of land use.

Zoning Ordinances—Local laws establishing building codes and usage regulations for properties in a specified area.

BIBLIOGRAPHY AND ADDITIONAL RESOURCES

Black's Law Dictionary, Fifth Edition. St. Paul, MN: West Publishing Company, 1979.

Coughlin, George Gordon, *Law for the Layman*. New York, NY: Harper & Row, 1975.

Gifis, Steven H., *Law Dictionary*. New York, NY: Barron's Educational Series, Inc., 1975.

Glossary of Legal Terminology: Law and the Courts. Chicago, IL: American Bar Association.

Oceana's Legal Almanac Series. New York, NY: Oxford University Press.

Webster's New World Dictionary. New York, NY: Simon & Schuster, 1981.